THE BEST OF BRIDGE

THE
BEST OF BRIDGE

An introduction to the Wohlin Collection
by

Victor Mollo

and

Eric Jannersten

FABER & FABER
3 QUEEN SQUARE
LONDON

First published 1973
by Faber and Faber Limited
3 Queen Square, London WC1
Reprinted 1974
Printed in Great Britain
by Unwin Brothers Limited
The Gresham Press, Old Woking Surrey

ISBN 0 571 10154 2

Introduction

To the public at large the name of Jan Wohlin is almost unknown. To the *cognoscenti* it stands for bridge expertise of the highest order.

When still in his early twenties, "the fat boy", his nickname among internationals, was already recognised as one of the world's half-dozen greatest card players, ranking in wizardry with America's Howard Schenken, Britain's Adam Meredith and Austria's Karl Schneider.

But Wohlin is something more than a magician. He is, above all, an ardent collector of the *objets d'art* of bridge—hands of outstanding interest.

With many treasures, gathered over the years; unsurpassed in technique, and a rare gift for penetrating in one sharp thrust to the heart of the trickiest problem, Jan Wohlin stands in a class by himself as a bridge analyst.

How is it then, that only the experts know of him? The answer is that Wohlin leads a secluded life in Sweden and writes only in Swedish—and who, outside Sweden, speaks Swedish?

Four Wohlin hands, written up in English, appear regularly in the monthly Bulletin of the IBPA—the International Bridge Press Association. It is by no means the least attractive feature of this specialised publication, but the readership is confined almost entirely to professionals—journalists, editors, tournament directors. On occasion, I have featured Wohlin hands in London's *Evening Standard*, but by and large, connoisseurs apart, no one outside Sweden has viewed until now any part of the Wohlin collection.

The purpose of this book is to present to the public exhibits which only a handful of experts have been privileged to see before, and many others, too, which no expert, not even in Sweden, has viewed as yet.

The reader will come across no freaks in these pages. Ordinary hands and everyday situations make the background for every example. Yet there isn't a single cliché, for to every deal Wohlin imparts some new and unexpected twist, and wrapped in each one is a message. As the reader unfolds it, he will learn, without fail, something he didn't know before.

In keeping with the originality of the material, the presentation is novel in conception and in design. That is the distinctive contribution of Eric Jannersten.

The *Official Encyclopedia of Bridge* describes Jannersten as "one of the leading bridge personalities of Europe". For more than two decades he has stood in the forefront of the international stage. Author and journalist, editor and publisher, player, commentator and organiser, he has starred in many parts. None has been more important or more successful than that of founder and director of a bridge school through which he has guided over 200,000 pupils.

With his unique qualifications and Swedish background, Jannersten was ideally suited to help me in presenting the Wohlin Collection to the world at large. So I sought eagerly his collaboration. I was motivated also by an urge to exploit what I can only describe as "the Jannersten Method".

Possessed of the born teacher's flair for imparting knowledge, Eric Jannersten sets every hand in a novel frame of his own design, sending out its message with unmistakable clarity. First the hand is misplayed. Only then, when the lessons of the error have been absorbed, is the correct play explained.

No hand is played badly. On the contrary, a skilful player is always at the wheel and his technique is good—up to a point. He slips, it is true, but that is only because some little thing escapes his notice and so he leaves a relevant factor out of account.

All players err. This isn't primarily due to lack of technique, still less to inexperience. The fault lies usually in failing to seize every available inference, and the surest way not to have the same lapse next time is to find out what caused it the time before. Therein lies the key to the Jannersten method. The student, and the post-graduate, too, is allowed to play back the record of his mental processes and to see for himself just when and where he went wrong. Then he is less likely to make the same mistake again.

The best of players will fail in some of the hundred and one hands which follow. That is as it should be, for one can learn only from mistakes, and though all mistakes are instructive, one's own, if taken to heart, are more profitable than other people's. Their's are, somehow, so much less important.

There is much bridge to learn from a study of the Wohlin Collection. There was much to learn in writing about it. And if, as I hope and believe, the reader enjoys viewing the exhibits as much as I have enjoyed presenting them, a truly good time will have been had by all.

Victor Mollo

Catalogue

Every hand in the Wohlin Collection is presented in three parts.

The first takes the classical form of a Quiz and asks the reader how he should play to make the contract or to break it, if he is defending.

Sometimes all four hands are on view from the start. This is not because a double-dummy problem is afoot, but because the bidding and the lead, or early play, pinpoint every card that matters and the test of skill lies in assessing correctly the chances and finding the winner.

For the next step the reader turns overleaf to the Aftermath. If he made a slip, he now sees the sorry sequel. Forewarned is forearmed. The Jannersten method shows him not only where, but above all why he went wrong and helps him to avoid the same error in future.

Now comes the last phase. The second best play is followed by the best. The contract is made—or broken—the lesson is learned and a hundred and one hands have happy endings.

The bidding is always simple and straightforward, and is given only to set the scene for the play. Systems don't come into it, and for the sake of convenience, all opening bids of 1 NT follow the same pattern—weak (12–14) non-vulnerable and strong (16–18) vulnerable.

YOUR MOVE

Dealer West: Love All

♠ K64
♡ A
◇ AKQJ9
♣ J964

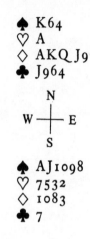

♠ AJ1098
♡ 7532
◇ 1083
♣ 7

West	North	East	South
Pass	1 ◇	Pass	1 ♠
Pass	3 ♣	Pass	3 ♠
Pass	4 ♠		

CONTRACT 4 ♠ : LEAD ♡ Q

North's leap to 3 ♣ was a little dashing and maybe South should have contented himself with 3 ◇, but there was nothing wrong with the contract.

At trick two declarer led dummy's ♠ 4, inserting the ♠ 8 when East followed with the ♠ 2. West's card was the ♠ 3.

Sitting South, how do you continue?

THE AFTERMATH

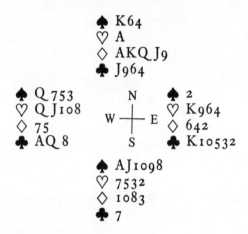

South led a second trump to dummy's king, intending to repeat the finesse. When East showed out, he sat back with a jolt, for if he played another trump, he would have three heart losers.

Hoping for the best, declarer came back to his hand with the ◊ 10, ruffed a heart and led out dummy's diamonds. West ruffed on the third round and South was left with three more losers, two hearts and a club.

HAPPY ENDING

West's defence was brilliant, but South should have made his contract for all that. Having finessed successfully—or so it seemed—against East, he should have then finessed against West! After making a trick with the ♠ 8, he should have run the ♠ 9. By all means let East win, if he can. Declarer can't be forced, for there is still a trump in dummy and all is well.

As it is, South makes an overtrick.

YOUR MOVE

Dealer South: Love All

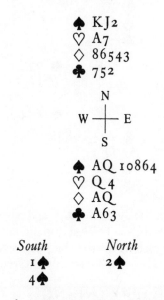

♠ KJ2
♥ A7
♦ 86543
♣ 752

N
W — E
S

♠ AQ10864
♥ Q4
♦ AQ
♣ A63

South	*North*
1 ♠	2 ♠
4 ♠	

CONTRACT 4♠: LEAD ♣10

There was a time when North would have responded 1NT, for a direct raise would have promised four-card support. Today most experts will bid 2♠. The pre-emptive value of the bid makes up for the fourth spade. Besides, when all is said and done, North doesn't like notrumps at all, so why say something you don't mean?

East plays the ♣J on West's ♣10.

What should be South's plan of campaign?

THE AFTERMATH

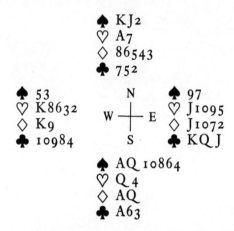

♠ K J 2
♡ A 7
◇ 8 6 5 4 3
♣ 7 5 2

♠ 5 3   N   ♠ 9 7
♡ K 8 6 3 2   W — E   ♡ J 1 0 9 5
◇ K 9   ◇ J 1 0 7 2
♣ 1 0 9 8 4   S   ♣ K Q J

♠ A Q 1 0 8 6 4
♡ Q 4
◇ A Q
♣ A 6 3

South won the first trick with the ♣ A, and entering dummy with the ♠ J, finessed the ◇ Q. West won and put East in with a second club. After cashing his last club, East switched to the ♡ J and eventually declarer had to concede a heart for one down.

HAPPY ENDING

Declarer played for a straightforward 50–50 chance and he can do much better than that.

First he should lay down the ♠ A. If either defender shows out, then he must indeed bring off the diamond finesse. So long as the trumps are no worse than 3–1, however, there is no need to worry about the ◇ K.

At trick three, South plays the ◇ A, then the ◇ Q. Defenders will do their worst by taking two clubs and switching to a heart, but South is a move ahead. He ruffs a diamond, crosses to the ♠ J and ruffs another diamond. And the ♠ K is still in dummy to give access to the fifth diamond, declarer's tenth trick.

YOUR MOVE

Dealer South: Love All

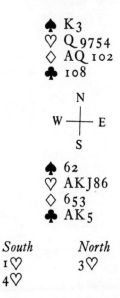

♠ K 3
♡ Q 9754
◇ AQ 102
♣ 108

```
        N
  W  ——  E
        S
```

♠ 62
♡ AKJ86
◇ 653
♣ AK 5

South	North
1♡	3♡
4♡	

CONTRACT 4♡ : LEAD ♠Q

Unless East has the ♠A and both the missing honours in diamonds, the defence has no chance. So declarer starts an odds-on favourite. The hottest favourites, however, have been known to go down.

To make certain of his contract—assuming no void in any suit—how should South play?

THE AFTERMATH

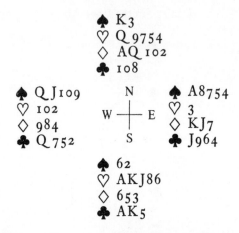

♠ K3
♡ Q 9754
♢ AQ 102
♣ 108

♠ Q J109   N   ♠ A8754
♡ 102   ♡ 3
         W ─┼─ E
♢ 984   ♢ KJ7
♣ Q 752   S   ♣ J964

♠ 62
♡ AKJ86
♢ 653
♣ AK5

South covered the ♠ Q with the ♠ K and East won. Then, to alert his partner to the importance of the diamond suit, he returned the ♠ 8, an unnecessarily high card and therefore a suit signal.

West promptly switched to a diamond and South had to lose two diamonds—and the contract.

HAPPY ENDING

To make his contract all South need do is to allow West to hold the first trick. Let him do his worst, which means, in effect, switch to a diamond.

Declarer goes up with the ♢ A, draws trumps, eliminates the clubs and throws East in with a spade.

East must either lead a diamond up to dummy or else concede a ruff and discard.

The key card is the ♠ K. It cannot take a trick, for it is clear from the lead that East must have the ♠ A. But precisely for that reason, East can be forced to take the lead when he least wants it.

YOUR MOVE

Dealer South: Both Vul:

♠ 952
♡ 842
◇ 863
♣ AQ 74

```
          N
     W ──┼── E
          S
```

♠ AK4
♡ AQ J109
◇ J4
♣ KJ2

South	North
1♡	1NT
4♡	

CONTRACT 4♡ : LEAD ◇2

No doubt South should have had a sixth heart for his bid, but he couldn't think of anything else to say and at least he had a hundred honours.

East won the first trick with the ◇A and returned another diamond to West's ◇K. Ruffing a third diamond with the ♡9, declarer laid down the ♡A to which both defenders followed.

Then, at trick five, South led the ♡Q.

Would you have played the same way?

THE AFTERMATH

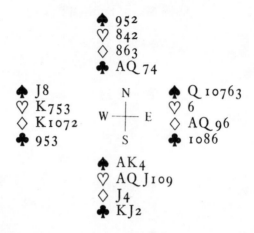

When East showed out on the second round of trumps, the temperature suddenly dropped and South felt acutely the need for that sixth trump.

Hoping for the best, he went on with trumps and all would have been well had West not found a fourth diamond. But he did, of course, and declarer couldn't stand being forced a second time.

West's ♡7 scored the setting trick.

HAPPY ENDING

To retain trump control, declarer should have led the ♡Q, not the ♡A. West plays low and South continues with the ♡J. If West wins, South has no further problems, for there is still a trump in dummy to deal with the diamonds. West, however, plays low again. Now South lays down the ♡A and leads clubs. So long as West follows three times, all is well.

YOUR MOVE

Dealer South: Love All

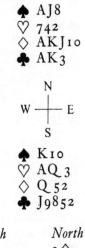

♠ AJ8
♡ 742
◇ AKJ10
♣ AK3

     N
W –––– E
     S

♠ K10
♡ AQ3
◇ Q52
♣ J9852

South	North
1♣	2◇
2NT	6NT

CONTRACT 6NT: LEAD ♠4

A most desirable contract and a favourable lead.

South played low from dummy and captured East's ♠Q with his ♠K. Next he led a club to dummy's ♣K, all following, and then the ♣A.

In the first three tricks declarer made two mistakes. What were they?

THE AFTERMATH

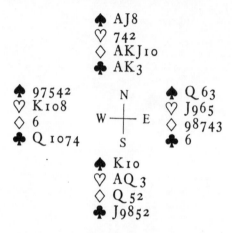

```
                    ♠ AJ8
                    ♡ 742
                    ◇ AKJ10
                    ♣ AK3
  ♠ 97542        N          ♠ Q63
  ♡ K108                    ♡ J965
  ◇ 6        W ─┼─ E        ◇ 98743
  ♣ Q1074         S         ♣ 6
                    ♠ K10
                    ♡ AQ3
                    ◇ Q52
                    ♣ J9852
```

After discovering the bad club break, there was nothing South could do, except to complain of bad luck.

HAPPY ENDING

As soon as dummy goes down, declarer can see that he will need four club tricks to bring his total to twelve. If the suit breaks nicely or if East turns up with four clubs, there is no problem. So, from the first, South's main concern should be the danger of finding four clubs in West's hand. Nothing else matters.

When all follow to the first club, South can make certain of his contract by running the ♣9. West won't oblige by covering, but declarer will play a third club, come back to his hand and drive out the ♣Q, setting up his long club.

There is just one snag. Declarer needs three entries to his hand—after taking a top club—and he has two only, the ♡A and the ◇Q. The ♡Q is an imponderable. To ensure a third entry he should go up with dummy's ♠J at trick one. If East covers, the ♠10 becomes an entry.

YOUR MOVE

Dealer South: E/W Vul:

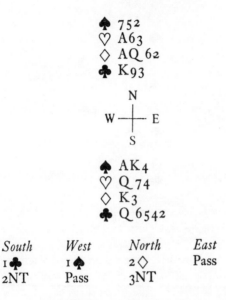

♠ 752
♡ A63
◇ AQ 62
♣ K93

N
W ──┼── E
S

♠ AK4
♡ Q 74
◇ K3
♣ Q 6542

South	West	North	East
1♣	1♠	2◇	Pass
2NT	Pass	3NT	

CONTRACT 3NT: LEAD ♠Q

South allowed the ♠Q to hold the first trick, won the spade continuation and turned his attention to clubs.

On his vulnerable overcall West was marked with the ♣A, so South led a low club towards dummy, going up with the ♣K on West's ♣8. His intention was to play low in clubs from both hands to the next trick in the hope that West had been dealt a doubleton ♣A.

Do you agree with his line of play?

THE AFTERMATH

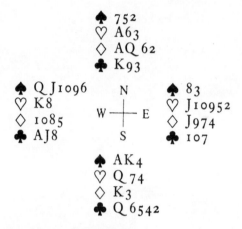

```
                    ♠ 752
                    ♡ A63
                    ◇ AQ 62
                    ♣ K93
  ♠ Q J1096        N        ♠ 83
  ♡ K8                      ♡ J10952
  ◇ 1085      W ─┼─ E       ◇ J974
  ♣ AJ8             S       ♣ 107
                    ♠ AK4
                    ♡ Q 74
                    ◇ K3
                    ♣ Q 6542
```

Unfortunately for South, West had two entries in clubs and was able to set up his spades before South could establish his clubs.

If the ♣ J and ♣ 10 had been reversed, all might have still been well—unless East had the presence of mind to unblock. That, however, is of academic interest. What matters is that South went down.

HAPPY ENDING

Declarer failed to profit by his good play at trick one. If East had a third spade, the suit wasn't dangerous, and if he hadn't, it was perfectly safe to let him win the first club.

South should have been content to cover West's ♣ 8 with dummy's ♣ 9, losing the trick to East. No doubt, East would return a heart. This declarer would win in dummy and the defence could do no more than take one spade, two clubs and one heart.

YOUR MOVE

Dealer South: Love All

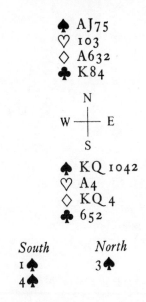

♠ AJ75
♡ 103
◇ A632
♣ K84

N
W —|— E
S

♠ KQ1042
♡ A4
◇ KQ4
♣ 652

South	*North*
1♠	3♠
4♠	

CONTRACT 4♠ : LEAD ♡6

Prospects were pleasing. If West had the ♣A or if the diamonds broke 3–3, there were ten cold tricks. And even if both were wrong, the defence might have communications problems.

The ♡6, ♡3, ♡K and ♡A made up the first trick. Trumps split 2–2, but for the rest declarer was admittedly unlucky, going one down. And yet, he should have made his contract.

How would you have played the hand?

THE AFTERMATH

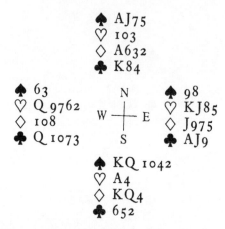

```
              ♠ AJ75
              ♡ 103
              ◇ A632
              ♣ K84

  ♠ 63           N          ♠ 98
  ♡ Q9762                   ♡ KJ85
  ◇ 108      W ─┼─ E        ◇ J975
  ♣ Q1073        S          ♣ AJ9

              ♠ KQ1042
              ♡ A4
              ◇ KQ4
              ♣ 652
```

When the diamonds failed to break, declarer ruffed the last
one and exited with a heart, hoping that East would win. West,
however, was wide awake. Going up promptly with the ♡Q, he
switched to the ♣Q.

HAPPY ENDING

Declarer made two mistakes at trick one, and though he
might have got away with the first one, the second proved
irremediable.

Even if East had the ♣A and the diamonds split 4–2, the
contract could be made—so long as East had the fourth
diamond.

After drawing trumps, declarer plays four rounds of diamonds, leaving East on play. As things are he can exit with a heart,
but had South allowed him to hold the first trick, he would be
forced at this point to lead a club up to dummy's ♣K or to
concede a ruff and discard.

To be really safe, South should have played dummy's ♡10
at trick one. On the ♡3, East, applying the Rule of Eleven,
might have played the ♡5, leaving West on play with the ♡6.
To avoid the club switch, South would be forced to win the
trick, bringing about the same position as before.

YOUR MOVE

Dealer South: Both Vul:

♠ 873
♡ 854
◇ AKJ4
♣ KQ5

```
        N
  W ——+—— E
        S
```

♠ AQ
♡ KJ7
◇ Q532
♣ J742

South	West	North	East
1◇	1♠	3◇	Pass
3NT			

CONTRACT 3NT: LEAD ♠J

Winning the first trick with the ♠Q, South led a low club to dummy's ♣K. West followed with the ♣6 and East with the ♣3.

Taking over South's hand, how do you continue?

THE AFTERMATH

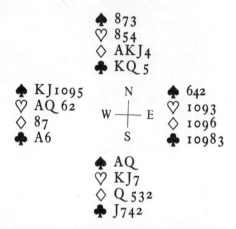

```
              ♠ 873
              ♡ 854
              ♢ AKJ4
              ♣ KQ5
♠ KJ1095          N          ♠ 642
♡ AQ62                       ♡ 1093
♢ 87       W ──┼── E         ♢ 1096
♣ A6              S          ♣ 10983
              ♠ AQ
              ♡ KJ7
              ♢ Q532
              ♣ J742
```

Declarer needed three club tricks for his contract, but was understandably apprehensive about his communications. So when the ♣K held, he continued with the ♣Q. Since the suit didn't break, South couldn't come to more than eight tricks.

HAPPY ENDING

Had the ♢5 and ♢4 been reversed, South would have had reason to play for the unlikely 3–3 club break. As things were, he had no excuse.

After the ♣K, he should have laid down the ♢AK. Once both defenders follow, he overtakes the ♢J with the ♢Q and leads clubs again towards dummy. West wins and drives out the ♠A, but the ♢5 provides an entry to the ♣J in the closed hand and all is well.

YOUR MOVE

Dealer South: Love All

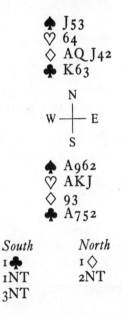

♠ J53
♡ 64
◇ AQJ42
♣ K63

```
        N
   W ──┼── E
        S
```

♠ A962
♡ AKJ
◇ 93
♣ A752

South	North
1♣	1◇
1NT	2NT
3NT	

CONTRACT 3NT: LEAD ♡5

Declarer captured East's ♡Q with his ♡K and led the ◇3. West played low and dummy's ◇J held the trick. Crossing back to his hand with the ♣A, declarer repeated the diamond finesse.

Do you agree with his play?

THE AFTERMATH

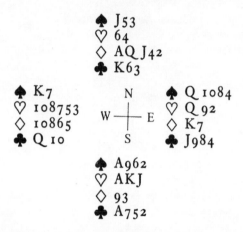

♠ J53
♡ 64
◇ AQJ42
♣ K63

♠ K7   ♠ Q1084
♡ 108753   ♡ Q92
◇ 10865   ◇ K7
♣ Q10   ♣ J984

♠ A962
♡ AKJ
◇ 93
♣ A752

East, who had ducked nonchalantly on the first round of diamonds, now came in with the ◇ K and returned a heart. With the ♣ K as his sole entry to dummy, declarer couldn't develop a third diamond trick and went down.

HAPPY ENDING

The damage was done at trick two. South can afford a 4–2 diamond break, but he cannot afford to use the ♣ K as an entry until the third diamond has been made good.

So, to preserve communications, he plays low from both hands on the first round. Now he has a second diamond as a link with dummy. He can take the finesse and whether it wins or loses, he has developed three diamond tricks—and the ♣ K is still there.

YOUR MOVE

Dealer South: Both Vul:

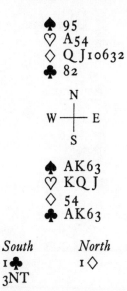

♠ 95
♡ A54
◇ QJ10632
♣ 82

```
        N
  W  ──┼── E
        S
```

♠ AK63
♡ KQJ
◇ 54
♣ AK63

South	North
1♣	1◇
3NT	

CONTRACT 3NT: LEAD ♡10

Assuming a humdrum, everyday distribution, do you expect declarer to make his contract?

What is your line of play?

THE AFTERMATH

```
              ♠ 95
              ♡ A54
              ◇ Q J10632
              ♣ 82
♠ J842           N           ♠ Q 107
♡ 1098                       ♡ 7632
◇ A987      W ─┼─ E          ◇ K
♣ J9             S           ♣ Q 10754
              ♠ AK63
              ♡ KQ J
              ◇ 54
              ♣ AK63
```

Declarer won the first trick in his hand with the ♡ J and led
a diamond to dummy's ◇ Q. Coming in with his bare ◇ K,
East returned a heart to South's ♡ Q. The ◇ J scored the next
trick, but with only one entry in dummy, there was no way of
developing another trick in diamonds. Complaining bitterly of
his bad luck, declarer went one down.

HAPPY ENDING

Far from being unlucky, South found a particularly favourable distribution. Against the more likely 3–2 diamond break,
he would have stood no chance, for of course he would be
allowed to win the first diamond and thereafter the entry
problem would prove insurmountable.

Declarer's only hope is to find a singleton honour, as above,
or else the ◇AK bare. In either case he makes his contract by
playing low from dummy the first time. There is no other hope.

YOUR MOVE

Dealer North: Both Vul:

```
        ♠ K5
        ♡ Q 63
        ◇ AK42
        ♣ AJ73
            N
        W ──┼── E
            S
        ♠ AQ 9642
        ♡ KJ9
        ◇ Q J6
        ♣ 8
```

South	North
—	1NT
3♠	4♣
4NT	5♡
6♠	

CONTRACT 6♠ : LEAD ♡4

By inference, North's 4♣ is a cue-bid, agreeing spades. If South is concerned only with finding the best game contract, he rebids 4♠. If he is good enough to envisage a slam, he goes on, as in this case.

East went up with the ♡A and returned the ♡8, West following with the ♡2.

Assuming that you win in your hand, which card do you play to trick three?

THE AFTERMATH

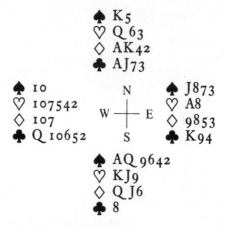

♠ K5
♡ Q 63
◇ AK42
♣ AJ73

♠ 10
♡ 107542
◇ 107
♣ Q 10652

N
W ─┼─ E
S

♠ J873
♡ A8
◇ 9853
♣ K94

♠ AQ 9642
♡ KJ9
◇ Q J6
♣ 8

South led a trump to dummy's king and another to his ace, discovering the 4–1 break. The only hope was to catch East's ♠ J by a trump reduction play, so South cashed the ♣ A and ruffed a club. Next he played the ◇ Q and crossed to dummy's ◇ K to ruff another club. Now he had the same length in trumps as East and all would have been well had the diamonds been divided 3–3. As it was, he couldn't afford to go back to dummy by overtaking the ◇ J, for that would leave East with the best diamond, and South had somehow to dispose of his heart or it would be ruffed. One down.

HAPPY ENDING

As soon as he sees dummy, declarer knows that only a 4–1 trump break can hurt him. So that should be his sole concern. There's no hope if West has four trumps, but if East is the culprit, all isn't lost. At trick three South leads, not a trump, but a club to the ♣ A, so as to ruff a club. This cannot cost a trick and is the key to trump reduction, should it be necessary.

The ♠ A comes next, then the ♠ K, not the other way round. Now declarer is in the right hand when he learns of the 4–1 trump break. He ruffs a second club and re-enters dummy

without having to overtake one diamond honour with another.
On the fourth diamond (the ♦A or ♦K), he throws a heart.
The lead is in dummy, where he wants it, and he sits with the
♠Q 9 poised over East's ♠ J8. Should both defenders follow
to the second round of trumps, no trump reduction is required
and the play is, of course, straightforward.

YOUR MOVE

This deal is more instructive with all four hands on view from the start.

Dealer South: Love All

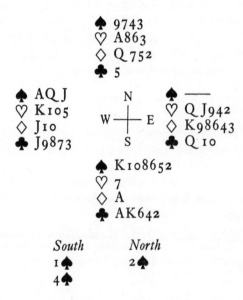

CONTRACT 4♠: LEAD ◇J

At trick two declarer laid down the ♣A, ruffed a club and led a trump, playing low when East showed out.

Do you agree with declarer's play?

What should West return at trick five?

This isn't a double-dummy problem, but every player—and every kibitzer—can draw sufficient inferences from the bidding and from the play to place the cards that matter.

THE AFTERMATH

When West won the fourth trick with the ♠J, he could place every card round the table. Since East had followed in clubs with the ♣10 and ♣Q, he could have no more. So South, who has shown six spades, started with five clubs. Could South have a losing diamond? Impossible, for he would have parked it on dummy's ♡A.

Thereupon West continued with the ♠A and ♠Q, giving up a certain trump trick to gain two clubs which South could no longer ruff in dummy. Good defence.

HAPPY ENDING

So long as declarer doesn't touch trumps, he cannot lose his contract. It is true that he can no longer come to twelve tricks, but neither can he fail to make ten. After ruffing a club at trick three, he cashes the ♡A and ruffs a heart in the closed hand. A second club ruff is followed by a diamond ruff. Now South cashes the ♣K and ruffs the last club in dummy.

If, at this point, declarer makes the right guess and ruffs a heart, rather than a diamond, he will come to eleven tricks, for West will find himself end-played in trumps.

YOUR MOVE

Dealer South: N/S Game

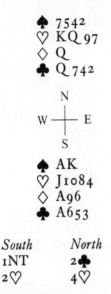

♠ 7542
♡ KQ97
♢ Q
♣ Q742

N
W —— E
S

♠ AK
♡ J1084
♢ A96
♣ A653

South	*North*
1NT	2♣
2♡	4♡

West leads the ♣J. Declarer plays low from dummy and East goes up with the ♣K.

Declarer wins, lays down the ♢A and ruffs a diamond. Coming back to the closed hand with the ♠A, he ruffs his second diamond loser. Next he plays the ♡K.

Would you have played the same way?

THE AFTERMATH

```
                    ♠ 7542
                    ♡ KQ 97
                    ◇ Q
                    ♣ Q 742

    ♠ Q 83              N              ♠ J1096
    ♡ A63                              ♡ 52
    ◇ K103       W ─┼─ E               ◇ J87542
    ♣ J1098             S              ♣ K

                    ♠ AK
                    ♡ J1084
                    ◇ A96
                    ♣ A653
```

West came in with the ♡ A and returned the ♣ 10. Declarer covered—not that it mattered—and East ruffed. West was bound to come to two more club tricks, so the contract was defeated.

HAPPY ENDING

A moment's pause before playing to trick one would have solved declarer's problem. Clearly the ♣ K must be a singleton, so why not let East hold the trick? Whatever he returns declarer wins and plays as before, ruffing his two diamond losers. When West is in with his ♡ A, he leads a club. Declarer plays low from dummy. If East ruffs, he ruffs a loser. If he doesn't, South wins with the ♣ A, draws trumps and concedes a club.

YOUR MOVE

Dealer South: Both Vul:

♠ K643
♡ KJ96
◇ AJ5
♣ J3

```
        N
   W ——+—— E
        S
```

♠ AQJ2
♡ AQ10852
◇ —
♣ K62

South	West	North	East
1♡	2◇	4♡	Pass
6♡			

CONTRACT 6♡: LEAD ◇K

When you see dummy, you probably wish that you were in 6♠, but unless you happen to be playing *canapé* and open 1♠, how do you get there?

Meanwhile, you are in 6♡. What is your plan of play?

THE AFTERMATH

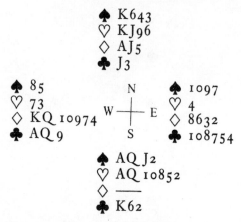

```
                    ♠ K643
                    ♡ KJ96
                    ◇ AJ5
                    ♣ J3
   ♠ 85              N            ♠ 1097
   ♡ 73                           ♡ 4
   ◇ KQ10974    W ─┼─ E           ◇ 8632
   ♣ AQ9             S            ♣ 108754
                    ♠ AQJ2
                    ♡ AQ10852
                    ◇ ──
                    ♣ K62
```

South threw a club on the ◇A, drew trumps, eliminated diamonds and cashed his spades. West was marked with the ♣A on his vulnerable overcall, so South brightly played low in clubs from both hands, hoping to find a singleton ♣A. It might have come off.

HAPPY ENDING

South played reasonably well, but he might have played better. Since the discard does him no good, he ruffs the ◇K in his hand at trick one and cashes his winners, ending in dummy. To keep a guard for his ◇Q, West must bare his ♣A and this is the three card end position:

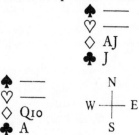

```
                    ♠ ──
                    ♡ ──
                    ◇ AJ
                    ♣ J
   ♠ ──              N
   ♡ ──
   ◇ Q10         W ─┼─ E
   ♣ A               S
```

West is thrown in with ♣A and must lead into dummy's ◇AJ.

YOUR MOVE

Dealer South: N/S Vul:

♠ K83
♥ KQ 6
♦ J103
♣ AKJ8

```
        N
  W ——+—— E
        S
```

♠ AQ
♥ A103
♦ AK842
♣ 753

South	North
1NT	6NT

CONTRACT 6NT: LEAD ♥2

Scientists might have conjured up several rounds of bidding to reach this very obvious contract. Playing Baron (the 1NT would then be weak, but let that pass), North would bid 2NT, a conventional response calling on South to show his four-card suit—or suits. That would have enabled the partnership to find a 4–4 fit, had there been one.

Meanwhile, there is nothing wrong with 6NT. How do you set about it?

THE AFTERMATH

```
              ♠ K83
              ♡ KQ 6
              ◇ J103
              ♣ AKJ8
  ♠ 107           N          ♠ J96542
  ♡ 9752      W —┼— E        ♡ J84
  ◇ Q9765         S          ◇ —
  ♣ 62                       ♣ Q1096
              ♠ AQ
              ♡ A103
              ◇ AK842
              ♣ 753
```

South won the first trick in dummy and led the ◇ J, expecting to make all thirteen tricks if East turned up with the ◇ Q. When East showed out, he needed the club finesse for twelve and when that failed too, he began to work out the odds against the appalling distribution of which he was the victim. And yet the story should have had a . . .

HAPPY ENDING

South can stand a 5–0 diamond break and since he is not in a grand slam, he might have given it a thought. At trick two he crosses to the closed hand with a spade and leads a low diamond. West plays low, dummy's J wins and East's void comes to light. Another spade is followed by another low diamond and West is helpless.

Note that if declarer is careless and plays low from dummy at trick one, East's ♡ J will kill a vital entry to the diamonds.

Needless to say, should East turn up with all five diamonds, it will present no problem. The ◇ J will fall to the ◇ Q, but the ◇ 9 will then be subject to a straightforward finesse.

YOUR MOVE

Since East can place, while South, a born pessimist, can guess every card, as soon as dummy goes down, the distribution holds no secrets. So let us look at all four hands from the start.

Dealer South: Both Vul:

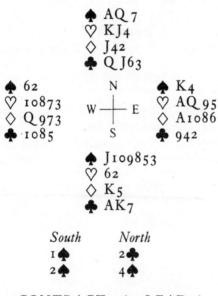

```
              ♠ AQ7
              ♡ KJ4
              ◇ J42
              ♣ QJ63
  ♠ 62            N        ♠ K4
  ♡ 10873                  ♡ AQ95
  ◇ Q973      W—+—E        ◇ A1086
  ♣ 1085          S        ♣ 942
              ♠ J109853
              ♡ 62
              ◇ K5
              ♣ AK7
```

South	North
1 ♠	2 ♣
2 ♠	4 ♣

CONTRACT 4♠: LEAD ◇3

On a heart opening declarer would have stood no chance. But what are the prospects now that West has led a diamond? Which side do you back?

THE AFTERMATH

It looks as if declarer must win, for after losing a diamond and a trump, he will be able to park a heart on dummy's fourth club. But East is there too. He knows from the bidding that South must have the ♢ K and from the lead that West has the ♢ Q. He would have hardly led the ♢ 3 from four small diamonds, but if he has, there is no hope anyway.

So, at trick two, East plays the ♢ 10, the grievous crime of "finessing against partner". When East comes in with his ♠ K, he underleads the ♢ A, putting West on play with the ♢ Q. Now a heart through dummy yields the defence two more tricks.

HAPPY ENDING

South, too, should be on the alert. His one concern must be to prevent West from gaining the lead, and as it happens, this presents no problem. All declarer need do is to put up dummy's ♢ J at trick one. Whether East wins or not is now immaterial.

YOUR MOVE

Dealer South: Love All

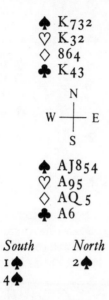

♠ K732
♡ K32
◇ 864
♣ K43

```
        N
  W ——+—— E
        S
```

♠ AJ854
♡ A95
◇ AQ5
♣ A6

South	North
1 ♠	2 ♠
4 ♠	

CONTRACT 4♠ : LEAD ♣Q

South won in his hand and led a trump to dummy's King, then another trump. East showed out, so South went up with the ♠A, cashed the ♣K and ruffed a club. Next he cashed the ♡A and ♡K, and put West on play with the ♠Q.

Would you have played the same way?

THE AFTERMATH

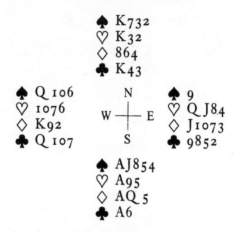

♠ K732
♡ K32
◇ 864
♣ K43

♠ Q 106   N   ♠ 9
♡ 1076   W ─┼─ E   ♡ Q J84
◇ K92   ◇ J1073
♣ Q 107   S   ♣ 9852

♠ AJ854
♡ A95
◇ AQ 5
♣ A6

South hoped that West wouldn't have a third heart or else that it would be the ♡Q, so that he would remain on play.

Alas, West had a heart as an exit card and East produced the ♡Q. Now the ◇J through the closed hand proved fatal.

HAPPY ENDING

South had the right idea, but he conceived it too late.

First, before touching trumps, he should eliminate the clubs, then the hearts. East will attack with his ◇J, but declarer will be one move ahead. Going up with the ◇A, he will lead a spade to the king and another spade, intending to finesse. Should West win, he will have to lead a diamond up to South's ◇Q5 or concede a ruff and discard. When East shows out, South wins and throws West in with the ♠Q. Again West is helpless.

YOUR MOVE

Dealer West: N/S Vul:

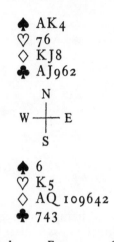

♠ AK4
♥ 76
♦ KJ8
♣ AJ962

```
        N
W ——+—— E
        S
```

♠ 6
♥ K5
♦ AQ 109642
♣ 743

West	North	East	South
1♠	1NT	Pass	3NT
4♡	Pass	Pass	5◇

CONTRACT 5◇ : LEAD ♠Q

An unusual sequence, but the North-South bidding isn't open to criticism. South, who must have given a thought to bidding 4NT over 4♡, feels greatly relieved when he sees dummy. On a heart lead defenders would surely take the first five or six tricks.

In diamonds there are ten top tricks. Where does declarer find the eleventh?

THE AFTERMATH

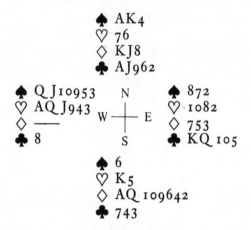

♠ AK4
♡ 76
◊ KJ8
♣ AJ962

♠ QJ10953   N   ♠ 872
♡ AQJ943   W ─┼─ E   ♡ 1082
◊ —   S   ◊ 753
♣ 8   ♣ KQ105

♠ 6
♡ K5
◊ AQ109642
♣ 743

South went up with dummy's ♠ K, crossed to his hand with a trump and led a club to the ♣ A. Next he discarded a club on the ♠ A, ruffed a spade and exited with his last club.

Declarer's hope was that West would be thrown in with the ♣ K and forced to lead a heart or to concede a ruff and discard. East, however, took the trick and returned a heart. One down.

HAPPY ENDING

West's bidding suggested twelve cards in the majors, so South's plan wasn't very promising. He had a much better chance, but he missed it at trick one.

West should be allowed to hold the first trick. Whatever he does next, South throws two clubs on the ♠ AK, cashes the ♣ A and ruffs a club. With three trump entries to dummy he can ruff two more clubs and get back to enjoy the ♣ 2 as his eleventh trick.

YOUR MOVE

Dealer South: Love All

```
            ♠ A1042
            ♡ AQ J7
            ◇ 63
            ♣ 742
                N
          W ——+—— E
                S
            ♠ 63
            ♡ K108643
            ◇ AJ
            ♣ AQ 5
```

South	North
1♡	3♡
4♡	

CONTRACT 4♡ : LEAD ♠Q

On the face of it, 3NT is obviously a superior contract, for there are nine top tricks against any lead and distribution. But how or why should anyone bid notrumps?

This is one of those cases where all the best players will find themselves in the second best contract.

How should South play to make it?

THE AFTERMATH

```
                    ♠ A1042
                    ♡ AQ J7
                    ◇ 63
                    ♣ 742

   ♠ Q J98          N          ♠ K75
   ♡ 2                         ♡ 95
   ◇ Q 974     W ──┼── E       ◇ K10852
   ♣ K1086          S          ♣ J93

                    ♠ 63
                    ♡ K108643
                    ◇ AJ
                    ♣ AQ 5
```

South went up with the ♠ A, drew trumps and ducked a diamond into West's hand. Coming on play at the next trick with the ♠ K, East switched to a club, and when the finesse failed, declarer conceded defeat.

HAPPY ENDING

In effect, South pinned all his hopes on the club finesse. An end-play against West was surely more promising.

To keep East out of the lead, South should allow the ♠ Q to hold the first trick. East cannot afford to overtake, for that would expose West to a marked finesse. Declarer wins the next trick, no doubt a second spade, and leads a diamond, inserting the ◇ J. Whatever West does next, South cashes the ◇ A, ruffs a spade and going back to dummy with a trump, leads the ♠ 10 (dummy's last spade), throwing on it his ♣ 5.

West must lead a club into South's ♣ AQ or else a diamond, conceding a ruff and discard.

YOUR MOVE

Dealer South: E/W Vul:

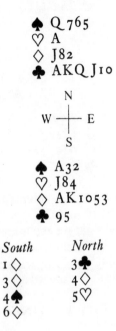

♠ Q 765
♡ A
♢ J82
♣ A K Q J 10

```
        N
  W ――――――― E
        S
```

♠ A 3 2
♡ J 8 4
♢ A K 10 5 3
♣ 9 5

South	North
1 ♢	3 ♣
3 ♢	4 ♢
4 ♠	5 ♡
6 ♢	

CONTRACT 6♢ : LEAD ♡K

This looks like an eminently good contract, especially without
a spade lead which might have proved embarrassing.

At trick two South led dummy's ♢ 2, inserting from the
closed hand the ♢ 10, which held the trick.

As he continued with the ♢ A South had high hopes of
making all thirteen tricks with: five trumps, the ♠ A, the ♡ A,
a heart ruff and five clubs.

Do you agree with declarer's play?

THE AFTERMATH

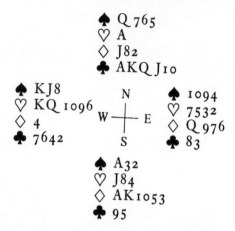

```
                    ♠ Q 765
                    ♡ A
                    ◇ J82
                    ♣ AKQ J10
    ♠ KJ8              N           ♠ 1094
    ♡ KQ 1096                      ♡ 7532
    ◇ 4          W ──┼── E         ◇ Q 976
    ♣ 7642                         ♣ 83
                     S
                    ♠ A32
                    ♡ J84
                    ◇ AK1053
                    ♣ 95
```

On the ◇ A, at trick three, West showed out and all at once the thirteen tricks shrank to eleven.

Declarer ruffed a heart and set about the clubs. East unfortunately, ruffed on the third round, and since he had a natural trump trick anyway, it wouldn't have helped South to over-ruff. So he shed his ♡ J and later conceded a spade.

HAPPY ENDING

Declarer was on the right track when he embarked at once on the trump finesse, and had it lost, all would have been well. Alas, it won and now declarer lost trump control, which was fatal.

At trick two, South should lead the ◇ J. It is a finesse, in a sense, for he intends to run it. But whether East covers or not, South plays low. Thereafter, unless all five trumps are in the same hand, no one can hurt him. Whatever East returns, South wins, ruffs a heart and draws trumps.

To retain trump control declarer must make sure of losing the trump finesse—even if it's right!

YOUR MOVE

Dealer South: Both Vul:

♠ 64
♡ 83
♢ J10753
♣ Q1083

```
        N
W ——+—— E
        S
```

♠ AKJ
♡ A106
♢ AQ4
♣ AKJ6

South	North
2♣	2♢
3NT	

CONTRACT 3NT: LEAD ♡4

East was allowed to win the first trick with the ♡Q. The ♡9 came back and again South played low. West won with the ♡J and continued with a third heart to South's ♡A, East following with the ♡5.

A successful finesse in diamonds or in spades would yield declarer his ninth trick. Which suit should it be?

To give himself every chance, South first laid down the ♢A, in case West had a singleton ♢K. Then he cashed the ♠A to allow for the bare ♠Q. Nothing happened, so he crossed to dummy with a club and took the spade finesse.

Can declarer do better?

THE AFTERMATH

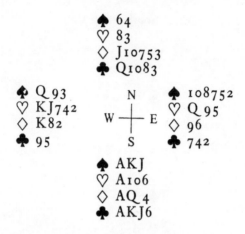

```
              ♠ 64
              ♡ 83
              ◇ J10753
              ♣ Q1083

♠ Q93            N            ♠ 108752
♡ KJ742     W ──┼── E       ♡ Q95
◇ K82            S            ◇ 96
♣ 95                         ♣ 742

              ♠ AKJ
              ♡ A106
              ◇ AQ4
              ♣ AKJ6
```

West came in with the ♠Q and cashed two more hearts to break the contract.

HAPPY ENDING

The lead of the ♡4, as also East's return of the ♡9 at trick two, indicated that West had started with a five-card suit. That wasn't dangerous. South should have won the second heart, cashed his two top clubs and exited with a heart.

West can cash two hearts. Throwing three diamonds from dummy, declarer will discard a diamond and a club from his own hand. But what will West do when he has no more hearts? A spade or a diamond will present declarer immediately with his ninth trick.

Should West have a third club, South will have the chance as before of taking a successful finesse.

YOUR MOVE

Dealer West: Love All

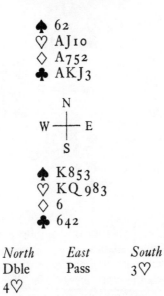

♠ 62
♡ A J 10
◇ A752
♣ A K J 3

N
W —— E
S

♠ K853
♡ K Q 983
◇ 6
♣ 642

West	North	East	South
1 ♠	Dble	Pass	3♡
Pass	4♡		

CONTRACT 4♡ : LEAD ◇K

South surveyed his prospects with satisfaction. If every card were in the right place, he could make twelve tricks. But, of course, West almost certainly had the ♠ A and the clubs were an unknown quantity.

Wasting no time, South went up with dummy's ◇ A and led a spade, so as to prepare for a spade ruff in dummy.

Would you have played the same way ?

THE AFTERMATH

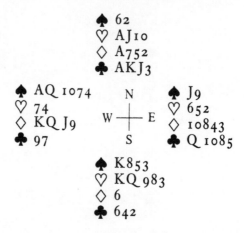

East won the second trick with the ♠ 9 and returned a trump. Another spade and another trump followed, declarer winning in his hand to ruff a spade.

Crossing back with a diamond ruff, South drew the last trump and tried the club finesse. The diamond return forced his sole remaining trump and there was no tenth trick to be had anywhere.

HAPPY ENDING

Admittedly, South was unlucky with the clubs, but then he didn't need any luck in the first place.

The hand lends itself perfectly to a dummy reversal. Forgetting all about spades, South ruffs a diamond in his hand at trick two, goes over to dummy first with the ♣ K, then with the ♣ A, and ruffs two more diamonds. Having collected six tricks, he exits with his last club and no one can prevent him from ruffing dummy's ♣ 3 with one of his honours.

Dummy's ♡ AJ10 will score the last three tricks.

YOUR MOVE

Dealer South: Love All

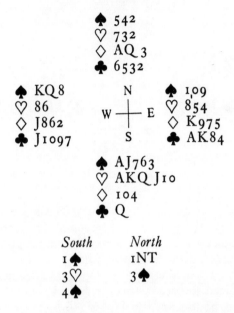

	♠ 542	
	♡ 732	
	◇ AQ 3	
	♣ 6532	

♠ KQ8	N	♠ 10 9
♡ 86	W ─┼─ E	♡ 854
◇ J862	S	◇ K975
♣ J1097		♣ AK84

	♠ AJ763	
	♡ AKQJ10	
	◇ 104	
	♣ Q	

South	*North*
1♠	1NT
3♡	3♠
4♠	

CONTRACT 4♠ : LEAD ♣J

East goes up with the ♣K and returns another club. South ruffs.

Which side will you back, declarer or the defence?

You can take up South's cards or seat yourself West. The choice is yours.

Which shall it be?

THE AFTERMATH

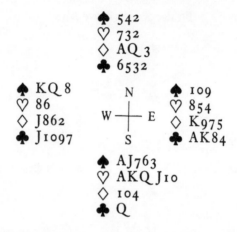

This hand came up in a French Championship. In one room South laid down the ♠ A and led a second spade. Winning with the ♠ Q, West cashed the ♠ K, removing dummy's last trump, and switched to a diamond. One down.

In the other room, South led a low spade away from his ♠ A. East was forced to overtake West's ♠ 8 and continued with another club. South ruffed again, laid down the ♠ A and led out his hearts. West couldn't gain by ruffing with his master trump and South was able to discard dummy's two losing diamonds. Contract made.

HAPPY ENDING

When, at trick three, South leads a low trump, West has the foresight to go up with an honour and so remains on play. A diamond through dummy's ◇ AQ 3 puts the defence one move ahead.

Did you back the winning side ?

YOUR MOVE

Dealer South: N/S Vul:

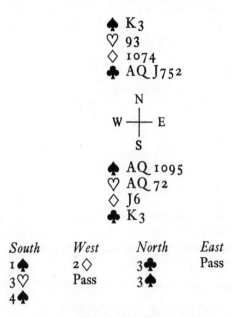

♠ K3
♡ 93
♢ 1074
♣ AQ J752

```
        N
   W ——+—— E
        S
```

♠ AQ 1095
♡ AQ 72
♢ J6
♣ K3

South	West	North	East
South	*West*	*North*	*East*
1♠	2♢	3♣	Pass
3♡	Pass	3♠	
4♠			

CONTRACT 4♠ : LEAD ♢K

West led out the three top diamonds, East following. South ruffed on the third round and looked for a safe way to make ten tricks. Nothing startling suggested itself, so he led a trump to dummy's king, then another towards the closed hand. East followed with the ♠4 and ♠7.

Would you have played the same way?

THE AFTERMATH

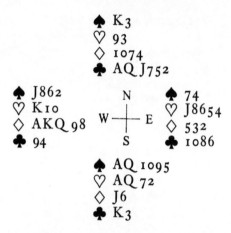

♠ K3
♡ 93
♦ 1074
♣ AQ J752

♠ J862
♡ K10
♦ AKQ98
♣ 94

N
W ─┼─ E
S

♠ 74
♡ J8654
♦ 532
♣ 1086

♠ AQ 1095
♡ AQ 72
♦ J6
♣ K3

When East showed out on the third round of trumps, things looked black. Having been forced once, South couldn't afford to clear trumps, for he would then have to concede two more diamonds. So he played on clubs—and went two down just the same.

HAPPY ENDING

The 4–2 trump break was in accordance with the odds, but declarer could afford to lose a trump, so long as it was the first one, while a trump remained in dummy to deal with another diamond.

Having ruffed the third diamond, South should run the ♠ 10. Let East win, with a doubleton jack for all South cares. Should East have a fourth diamond to play, declarer ruffs in dummy, gets back to his hand with the ♡ A and draws trumps.

If the ♠ 10 holds, as it would do in this instance, it's simpler still and South makes eleven tricks.

YOUR MOVE

Dealer South: Both Vul:

♠ A642
♡ K52
◇ 108
♣ 8652

```
          N
     W ──┼── E
          S
```

♠ 9
♡ AQ 7643
◇ AK63
♣ AK

South	North
2♡	3♡
6♡	

CONTRACT 6♡ : LEAD ◇ 5

South's bidding was not very imaginative, and had there been a grand slam in the cards, he would have only had himself to blame.

Meanwhile, finding dummy with nothing to spare, he was satisfied to be in six. Now, even a 4–0 trump break wouldn't necessarily prove fatal.

To the first trick South played dummy's ◇ 8 and captured East's ◇ J with the ◇ K. Then he laid down the ♡ A to which all followed.

What was the right continuation?

THE AFTERMATH

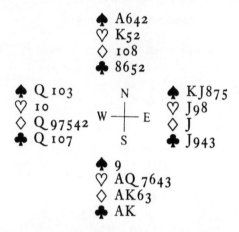

```
              ♠ A642
              ♡ K52
              ◇ 108
              ♣ 8652
♠ Q103          N        ♠ KJ875
♡ 10                     ♡ J98
◇ Q97542   W ─┼─ E       ◇ J
♣ Q107          S        ♣ J943
              ♠ 9
              ♡ AQ7643
              ◇ AK63
              ♣ AK
```

At trick three South led a heart to dummy's ♡ K, West
discarding a diamond. Declarer continued with the ◇ 10, but
East wasn't obliging enough to ruff. He threw a spade instead,
and now South's fate was sealed.

Helplessly, he ruffed a diamond with dummy's last trump,
but East over-ruffed and South was left with another diamond
to lose.

HAPPY ENDING

Having drawn one round of trumps, declarer should pause
to regroup. Before touching trumps again, he should cross to
the ♠ A and test the diamonds. If all follow, there are no
problems. As before, however, East throws a spade. But observe
the difference.

Declarer ruffs one of his two diamond losers with the ♡ K,
comes back to his hand with the ♣ A and ruffs his last diamond
with the ♡ 5. East over-ruffs, but the defence takes no other
trick.

YOUR MOVE

Dealer South: Love All

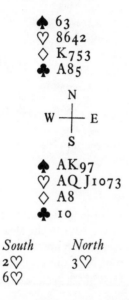

♠ 63
♡ 8642
♢ K753
♣ A85

N
W —— E
S

♠ AK97
♡ AQJ1073
♢ A8
♣ 10

South	*North*
2♡	3♡
6♡	

CONTRACT 6♡ : LEAD ♣4

This South seems to be an enormous cardholder, so he should have plenty of experience in coping with big distributional hands.

The first trick was won by dummy's ♣A. South continued with a trump on which East threw a diamond, a bad blow.

How should South proceed?

THE AFTERMATH

```
                    ♠ 63
                    ♡ 8642
                    ◇ K753
                    ♣ A85

♠ Q 104            N            ♠ J852
♡ K95                           ♡ ——
◇ Q 9         W —┼— E           ◇ J10642
♣ KJ742            S            ♣ Q 963

                    ♠ AK97
                    ♡ AQ J10073
                    ◇ A8
                    ♣ 10
```

Declarer went up with the ♡ A, cashed the two two spades and ruffed a spade. Coming back to the closed hand with a club ruff, he led his last spade, hoping for the best. Alas, West ruffed with the ♡ 9, in front of dummy, and there was still the ♡ K out to score the setting trick.

HAPPY ENDING

When West shows up with the ♠Q and ♠ 10, it's pretty obvious that he can have no more. With ♠Q J104, he would have opened a spade—instead of a speculative club. If declarer places East with four spades, as he should do, he only needs one more thing to bring home his slam—to find East with five diamonds.

Assuming that the distribution is as in the diagram above, declarer can make certain of his contract by playing out his winners.

When the last trump is played, dummy is left with ◇ K75. Declarer remains with the ♠ 7 and the ◇ A8.

Unable to retain the best spade and also three diamonds, East gives up.

YOUR MOVE

Matched-Pointed Pairs

Dealer South: E/W Vul:

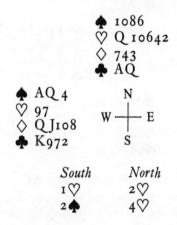

	♠ 1086	
	♡ Q 10642	
	◇ 743	
	♣ AQ	

♠ AQ 4	N
♡ 97	
◇ QJ108	W — E
♣ K972	S

South	*North*
1♡	2♡
2♣	4♡

CONTRACT 4♡ : LEAD ◇Q

On the ◇Q, East plays the ◇9 and declarer wins with the ◇A. Next come the ♡A and a heart to dummy's ♡Q. East follows the first time and then discards the ◇2.

To trick four declarer leads dummy's ♠8. East's card is the ♠2 and declarer himself plays the ♠7.

What prospects do you see for the defence?

THE AFTERMATH

```
                    ♠ 1086
                    ♡ Q 10642
                    ◇ 743
                    ♣ AQ
  ♠ AQ4              N            ♠ 532
  ♡ 97                            ♡ J
  ◇ QJ108        W ─┼─ E          ◇ K962
  ♣ K972             S            ♣ J10654
                    ♠ KJ97
                    ♡ AK853
                    ◇ A5
                    ♣ 83
```

West won the fourth trick (the ♠ 8) with his ♠Q, cashed the ◇Q and forced declarer with a third diamond. The defence scored one more trick in spades, but with the ♣ K under the ♣ A declarer duly made his contract.

What could poor West do about it?

HAPPY ENDING

West can make use of a vital piece of information which isn't available to declarer. He knows, and declarer doesn't, that the club finesse will succeed. So he wins the first spade not with the ♠Q, but with the ♠A, creating the impression that East has the ♠Q. Then he switches to a club.

Thinking that he doesn't need the club finesse and that he will be able to discard dummy's ♣Q on his fourth spade, declarer is likely to go up with the ♣A—and to go down in his contract.

At rubber bridge he wouldn't take the risk, but in a pairs event he would look very foolish making ten tricks if every other South made eleven.

YOUR MOVE

Dealer South: Love All

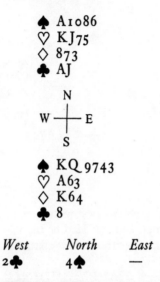

♠ A1086
♡ KJ75
◇ 873
♣ AJ

```
        N
   W ——+—— E
        S
```

♠ KQ9743
♡ A63
◇ K64
♣ 8

South	West	North	East
1♠	2♣	4♠	—

CONTRACT 4♠ : LEAD ♣K

Declarer won the first trick with the ♣A, ruffed the ♣J and drew trumps in two rounds, West having the singleton.

Next declarer cashed the two top hearts, crossed to his hand with a trump and exited with a heart.

Could declarer have done any better?

THE AFTERMATH

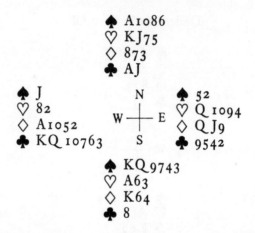

Declarer had done his best to give himself an extra chance, but it wasn't good enough. Had he thought a moment longer, he could have made certain of his contract.

HAPPY ENDING

The ♣ J is too precious to ruff, for it can be used as a certain throw-in card against West.

As before, declarer wins the first trick, draws trumps and cashes the ♡ A, then the ♡ K. Now comes the key play—the ♣ J on which South throws his third heart.

If West has no heart left, he must lead a diamond or concede a ruff and discard. If he has a heart, South covers in dummy and comes to a heart trick, no matter how the suit is divided.

YOUR MOVE

Dealer South: E/W Vul:

```
            ♠ A5
            ♡ 653
            ◇ J7654
            ♣ A54

            N
        W ──┼── E
            S

            ♠ 86
            ♡ AKQ42
            ◇ A10
            ♣ KQ73
```

South	*North*
1♡	1NT
2♣	3♡
4♡	

CONTRACT 4♡: LEAD ♠K

South won with the ♠A and continued with the ♡A and ♡K. West threw a spade on the second round, and with a certain trump loser, it became a question of not losing a club.

South laid down the ♣K, crossed to the ♣A and continued with a third club.

Could he have done any better?

THE AFTERMATH

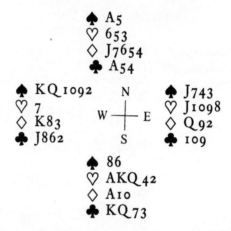

```
              ♠ A5
              ♡ 653
              ◇ J7654
              ♣ A54
♠ KQ1092      N       ♠ J743
♡ 7                   ♡ J1098
◇ K83      W ─┼─ E    ◇ Q92
♣ J862        S       ♣ 109
              ♠ 86
              ♡ AKQ42
              ◇ A10
              ♣ KQ73
```

East ruffed the third club, put West in with a spade and ruffed another club.

Everyone commiserated with South. He would have made his contract if the trumps hadn't been 4–1 or if the clubs had broken 3–3 or if East had the long clubs or if West hadn't turned up with an entry at the critical moment.

Four things out of four were wrong.

HAPPY ENDING

South could do nothing about the first three blows of fortune, but he could have averted the fourth. He had nothing to gain by winning the first spade. By playing low at trick one he would have cut communications between East and West, and unless East could ruff two clubs, he couldn't have broken the contract.

YOUR MOVE

Dealer South: Both Vul:

♠ A103
♡ 865
◇ 9642
♣ AQ7

```
        N
  W  ——+—— E
        S
```

♠ Q82
♡ A3
◇ AK1073
♣ K103

South	North
1◇	1♠
1NT	2NT
3NT	

CONTRACT 3NT: LEAD ♠5

Feeling that he had too much for a raise to 2◇ and not the right type of hand for a jump to 3◇, North compromised with a response of 1♠. This might have led to complications, but in the event, there was nothing wrong with the final contract.

Without looking for anything devilish in the distribution, how should South play?

THE AFTERMATH

```
                    ♠ A10 3
                    ♡ 8 6 5
                    ◇ 9 6 4 2
                    ♣ A Q 7
♠ J 9 7 5 4          N          ♠ K 6
♡ K 7 2                         ♡ Q J 10 9 4
◇ —            W ─┼─ E          ◇ Q J 8 5
♣ 9 6 5 4 2          S          ♣ J 8
                    ♠ Q 8 2
                    ♡ A 3
                    ◇ A K 10 7 3
                    ♣ K 10 3
```

Declarer played low from dummy at trick one and East, coming in with the ♠K, switched at once to a heart.

Not being blessed with second sight, South failed to bring in the diamonds without loss and went two down.

Just one more case of bad luck.

HAPPY ENDING

Since South cannot stand a heart switch, he should go up with the ♠A and keep East out of the lead. Fortunately, this presents no difficulty.

Having won the first trick with the ♠A, South leads dummy's ◇9. So long as East follows, all is well. Let West win, with a singleton perhaps. He can do no harm and four diamond tricks suffice for the contract.

If East covers, South wins, crosses to dummy and repeats the finesse.

Unless West has all four diamonds, the contract is unbeatable.

YOUR MOVE

Dealer South: Love All

```
        ♠ 642
        ♡ J73
        ◇ A1062
        ♣ A95

           N
       W ──┼── E
           S

        ♠ AKQ
        ♡ KQ4
        ◇ KQ84
        ♣ KQJ
```

CONTRACT 6NT: LEAD ♡10

Declarer played low from dummy. East went up with the
♡A and returned another heart to South's ♡K.

With eleven top tricks, it was clear that the contract would
hinge on bringing in the long diamond. So, without beating
about the bush, South led out the ◇K, then the ◇Q. If all
followed, he would spread his hand. If East showed out, he
would take the marked finesse against West's ◇J.

Could you improve on this play?

THE AFTERMATH

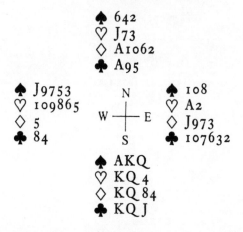

                              ♠ 642
                              ♡ J73
                              ◇ A1062
                              ♣ A95
    ♠ J9753   N   ♠ 108
    ♡ 109865   ♡ A2
    ◇ 5   W ——+—— E   ◇ J973
    ♣ 84   ♣ 107632
                              S
                              ♠ AKQ
                              ♡ KQ4
                              ◇ KQ84
                              ♣ KQJ

When West, not East, showed out on the second round of
diamonds, South surrendered, for there was nothing he could
do about it.

HAPPY ENDING

Declarer was wrong not to beat about the bush. The diamonds couldn't run away and, meanwhile, he could gather a
lot of useful information.

First, he takes a third round of hearts and sees East show
out. So West had five. Three rounds of spades tell the same
story. West is now marked with ten cards in the majors.
Should he fail to follow on the first or second club, he must
have two (or three) diamonds, so all is well. If he follows twice,
he cannot have more than one diamond. Now South leads a
diamond to dummy's ◇ A and continues with the ◇ 10, intending to run it unless East covers. If he does, South crosses
to dummy with the ♣ A and finesses against East's ◇ 9.

YOUR MOVE

Dealer South: Love All

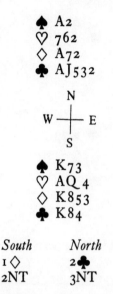

♠ A2
♡ 762
◇ A72
♣ AJ532

```
        N
   W ——+—— E
        S
```

♠ K73
♡ AQ4
◇ K853
♣ K84

South	North
1 ◇	2 ♣
2NT	3NT

CONTRACT 3NT: LEAD ♠Q

South allowed the ♠Q to hold. He won the spade continuation, laid down the ♣K and led a second club towards dummy.
Would you have played the same way?

THE AFTERMATH

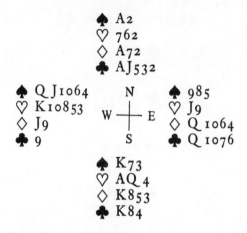

West showed out on the second club and the hand collapsed.

HAPPY ENDING

Since declarer needs four clubs for his contract, he should give that top priority.

If the suit breaks 3–2 or if West has four clubs, there is no problem. So South's main concern is to guard against four clubs with East. In that event his only hope is that West's singleton should be the ♣9 or ♣10—or, of course, the ♣Q.

The first spade is won in the closed hand. A low club to the ♣A is followed by a second club, South inserting the ♣8 unless East covers. If he does, declarer wins with the ♣K and concedes a club. He has now set up his ninth trick and the defence can do nothing about it.

YOUR MOVE

Dealer South: N/S Vul:

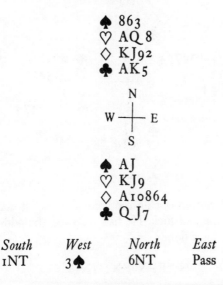

♠ 863
♡ AQ 8
◇ KJ92
♣ AK5

N
W —|— E
S

♠ AJ
♡ KJ9
◇ A10864
♣ QJ7

South	West	North	East
1NT	3♠	6NT	Pass

CONTRACT 6NT: LEAD ♠K

South's 1NT promised 16–18 points. So, over West's 3♠, North saw no reason to dilly-dally and jumped directly to 6NT.

When South caught his first glimpse of dummy he regretted that he hadn't opened 1◇. Then he shrugged his shoulders philosophically. If he found the ◇Q, he would make 6NT. If he did not, he would not have made 6◇.

Since West was marked with six or seven spades, East was likely to be longer than West in diamonds. Winning the first trick with the ♠A, South led a low diamond towards the table.

Have you any fault to find with this play?

THE AFTERMATH

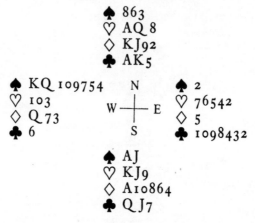

When East showed out on the second round of diamonds, South cursed his bad luck. He had followed the odds. What more could he have done?

HAPPY ENDING

All might have been well had South's second spade been the two or the three. He would have played low to trick one, for there would be nothing to gain by doing otherwise. The ♠J was different—or so it seemed. Yet that was an illusion. If South fails to find the ◇Q, he is lost anyway. Meanwhile, his best chance is to get a count on the other suits.

He plays low to the first trick and discovers, when he takes his ♠A, that West started with seven spades. The clubs follow and it comes to light that West had a singleton. The hearts come next and when West shows out on the third round, he can be counted for seven spades, two hearts and one club, hence three diamonds. South lays down the ◇A and finesses confidently.

Had West produced a second club or a third heart, South would have played for the diamonds to be 2–2. One more card from West in clubs or hearts, and the finesse would be taken against East.

YOUR MOVE

Dealer South: Love All

♠ 975**2**
♡ AQ 94
◇ K
♣ AK53

```
        N
   W ──┼── E
        S
```

♠ AQ
♡ KJ10863
◇ Q 6
♣ Q 7**2**

South	North
1 ♡	3 ♣
3 ♡	4 ♡
4 ♠	6 ♡

CONTRACT 6♡ : LEAD ♡5

Declarer cleared trumps in two rounds—East throwing the
◇ 2 the second time—and turned to the clubs. West discarded
the ◇9 on the third round.

How should declarer continue?

THE AFTERMATH

```
              ♠ 9752
              ♡ AQ 94
              ◇ K
              ♣ AK53
  ♠ K1063         N          ♠ J84
  ♡ 52                       ♡ 7
  ◇ AJ974     W ─┼─ E        ◇ 108532
  ♣ J8            S          ♣ 10964
              ♠ AQ
              ♡ KJ10863
              ◇ Q 6
              ♣ Q 72
```

When this hand came up in a match, one declarer bowed to fate and took the spade finesse like a man. One down.

"Doubtless, the result will be the same in the other room", remarked North consolingly. "It's hardly possible to keep out of a slam on our cards."

HAPPY ENDING

Declarer in the other room was, however, more resourceful. Feeling that the spade finesse wouldn't run away, he tried a pseudo end-play.

After ruffing the fourth club, he exited with a diamond—to be precise, the ◇Q, conveying the impression that he had no more.

Coming in with the ◇A, West was afraid to concede a ruff and discard, and kindly led a spade.

Yes, West should have known better. If South had a single-ton diamond, he must have three spades, so a ruff and discard wouldn't help him.

YOUR MOVE

Dealer South: Love All

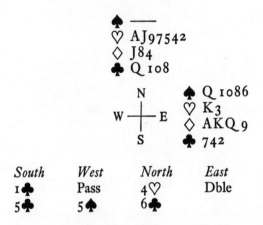

```
              ♠ —
              ♡ AJ97542
              ◇ J84
              ♣ Q 108
                        N        ♠ Q 1086
                                 ♡ K3
                   W  ─┼─ E      ◇ AKQ 9
                        S        ♣ 742
```

South	West	North	East
1♣	Pass	4♡	Dble
5♣	5♠	6♣	

CONTRACT 6♣: LEAD ◇3

East, whose double of 4♡ was primarily for a take-out, fancied his chances in defence and felt little temptation to sacrifice.

He won the first trick with the ◇Q and looked at the ceiling for inspiration.

What should he have played when he looked down again?

THE AFTERMATH

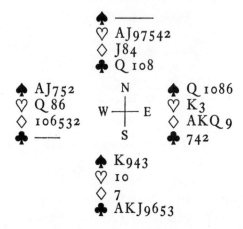

♠ ——
♡ AJ97542
◇ J84
♣ Q108

♠ AJ752   N   ♠ Q1086
♡ Q86 W——E ♡ K3
◇ 106532   ◇ AKQ9
♣ ——   S   ♣ 742

♠ K943
♡ 10
◇ 7
♣ AKJ9653

East found nothing helpful on the ceiling and he continued with the ◇A. South ruffed, crossed to dummy with the ♡A and ruffed a heart. He went back to the table with a trump and ruffed another heart. Next he drew trumps, ending in dummy, and counted four more heart tricks to bring his total to twelve.

HAPPY ENDING

East should have looked more carefully at the ceiling. He would have doubtless discovered that if South had two diamonds, he would lose another diamond anyway. And if he had two hearts, he would assuredly lose a heart. Even if he had a void in hearts, he couldn't cope. The one all-important consideration was to deny declarer access to dummy's hearts. So, at trick two, East should have played a spade, forcing South to ruff in dummy. Now, with three trumps to dummy's two, East would exercise long distance control over the hearts.

YOUR MOVE

Declarer West: Love All

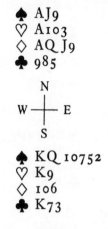

♠ AJ9
♡ A103
♢ AQ J9
♣ 985

```
        N
W ——┼—— E
        S
```

♠ KQ 10752
♡ K9
♢ 106
♣ K73

West	North	East	South
Pass	1 ♢	Pass	1 ♠
Pass	1NT	Pass	4 ♠

CONTRACT 4♠ : LEAD ♠4

Playing a weak (12–14) notrump, North's 1NT rebid promises 15–16 points. South has something to spare for his jump to game and need fear nothing in the post-mortem—so long as he makes it.

How should he set about it?

THE AFTERMATH

```
              ♠ A J 9
              ♡ A 10 3
              ◇ A Q J 9
              ♣ 9 8 5

  ♠ 6 4          N          ♠ 8 3
  ♡ J 8 6 4             ♡ Q 7 5 2
  ◇ 7 5 3    W ─┼─ E    ◇ K 8 4 2
  ♣ A Q 6 2      S          ♣ J 10 4

              ♠ K Q 10 7 5 2
              ♡ K 9
              ◇ 10 6
              ♣ K 7 3
```

Declarer drew trumps and ran the ◇ 10. East won and returned the ♣ J. South went down without batting the proverbial eyelid. His contract had a seventy-five per cent chance of success and as the French say, *la plus belle fille du monde ne peut donner que tout ce qu'elle a.*

Yes, but did she?

HAPPY ENDING

La plus belle fille greatly improves her chances by leading a heart at trick two and inserting the ♡ 9. West wins and does his worst by switching to a diamond. The ◇ A goes up. Next comes the ♡ K, a trump to dummy and the ♡ A, the ◇ 10 being shed from the closed hand. The ◇ Q follows for a ruffing finesse. Should West produce the ◇ K, it won't matter for he can do no harm.

If East turns up with both the ♡ Q and ♡ J, the other chances will remain unimpaired.

YOUR MOVE

Dealer West: N/S Vul:

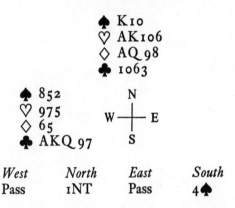

♠ K10		
♡ AK106		
◇ AQ98		
♣ 1063		

♠ 852   N
♡ 975   W —|— E
◇ 65   S
♣ AKQ97

West	*North*	*East*	*South*
Pass	1NT	Pass	4♠

CONTRACT 4♠ : LEAD ♣K

West leads out the three top clubs, declarer following all the way. East follows twice then discards the ♡ 4.

Which card should West lead at trick four? Any good reason for playing it, or is it a blind guess?

THE AFTERMATH

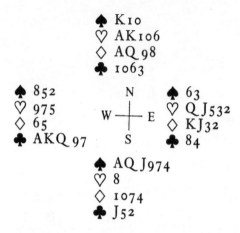

```
              ♠ K 10
              ♡ A K 10 6
              ◇ A Q 9 8
              ♣ 10 6 3

♠ 8 5 2            N            ♠ 6 3
♡ 9 7 5                         ♡ Q J 5 3 2
◇ 6 5        W ──┼── E          ◇ K J 3 2
♣ A K Q 9 7                     ♣ 8 4
                   S
              ♠ A Q J 9 7 4
              ♡ 8
              ◇ 10 7 4
              ♣ J 5 2
```

At trick four, West led the ◇ 6, the obvious thing to do. South knew perfectly well that West couldn't have the ◇ K, for he had passed as dealer and he had shown up already with five clubs, headed by the ♣AKQ. So he went up with dummy's ◇ A and played out his six trumps.

Reduced to three cards in the end game, East couldn't keep three hearts, as well as the ◇ K, and declarer scored the ♡ 10 as his tenth trick. That was a happy ending for South. But had West given the matter more thought, the defence, too, could have had a . . .

HAPPY ENDING

East would never have thrown a heart on West's third club, unless he had five hearts, for obviously he would try to keep as many hearts as there were in dummy.

If East had five hearts (or six), South couldn't have more than one. So West's first thought should have been to cut communications between declarer and his dummy.

The diamonds could wait—for a long time. The heart switch was urgent to kill any chance of a squeeze.

YOUR MOVE

Dealer West: Love All

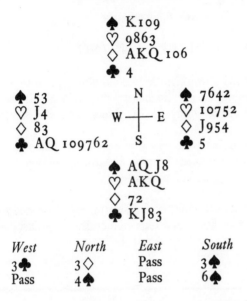

	♠ K109	
	♡ 9863	
	◇ AKQ 106	
	♣ 4	

	N	
♠ 53		♠ 7642
♡ J4	W E	♡ 10752
◇ 83		◇ J954
♣ AQ 109762	S	♣ 5

	♠ AQ J8
	♡ AKQ
	◇ 72
	♣ KJ83

West	North	East	South
3♣	3◇	Pass	3♠
Pass	4♠	Pass	6♠

CONTRACT 6♠: LEAD ♠5

The bidding isn't as strange as it looks. South had no intention of settling for anything less than a slam—so long as the opening lead ran up to his hand. But spades might prove better than notrumps, if North had a fit. It cost nothing to explore.

Are you on red or black, on declarer or on defenders?

Messieurs faites vos jeux

South wins the first trick in dummy and leads a club to his ♣J and West's ♣Q. Another trump comes back.

This is your last chance to place a bet.

Rien ne va plus.

THE AFTERMATH

Declarer wins the second trick in his hand, and ruffs a club with dummy's ♠ K.

Now we shall see for which side the story has a . . . ,

HAPPY ENDING

(a) East throws a heart on the second club, ruffed in dummy. South comes back to his hand with the ♡ A and plays one more round of trumps. West shows out and a diamond is thrown from dummy.

 South leads a second round of hearts and, when all follow, he can draw the last trump, discarding another diamond from dummy, and all is well—for South.

(b) On that second club, ruffed in dummy. East *under-ruffs*, keeping four hearts and four diamonds. Since East discards after dummy, declarer is now helpless.

YOUR MOVE

Dealer West: E/W Vul:

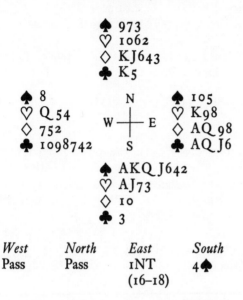

West	North	East	South
Pass	Pass	1NT	4♠
		(16–18)	

CONTRACT 4♠ : LEAD ♣10

East captured dummy's ♣K with the ♣A and continued with the ♣Q.

Declarer ruffed, drew trumps in two rounds and led the ◇10. West followed with the ◇2.

Should South make his contract?

THE AFTERMATH

East took the $\diamondsuit$ 10 with the $\diamondsuit$ Q and returned a heart. Declarer played low and West came in with the $\heartsuit$ Q, but the $\heartsuit$ K was now an easy prey for a finesse and defenders took no other tricks.

You still fancy the chances of the defence? Quite right. East didn't do himself justice.

HAPPY ENDING

By the time East comes in with the $\diamondsuit$ Q, he is what's known as a well-informed circle. He can place declarer with seven spades and one club. Since West followed with the $\diamondsuit$ 2, he must have three diamonds, for with a doubleton he would have started a high-low signal. So South's $\diamondsuit$ 10 was a singleton, leaving him with four hearts.

Having worked this out, East returns the $\diamondsuit$ 9. South can discard a heart for all the good it will do him. He will still have to open up the heart suit himself—and lose two hearts.

YOUR MOVE

Dealer South: Love All

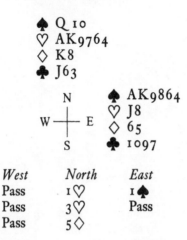

South	*West*	*North*	*East*
1 ◇	Pass	1 ♡	1 ♠
3 ◇	Pass	3 ♡	Pass
4 ♣	Pass	5 ◇	

CONTRACT 5 ◇ : LEAD ♠ 2

East won the first two tricks with the ♠ AK. West followed
with the ♠ 3 the second time, showing that he had started with
♠ J32.
How should East continue?

THE AFTERMATH

```
                    ♠ Q 10
                    ♡ AK9764
                    ◇ K8
                    ♣ J63

    ♠ J32           N           ♠ AK9864
    ♡ Q532      W ──┼── E       ♡ J8
    ◇ 972           S           ◇ 65
    ♣ Q82                       ♣ 1097

                    ♠ 75
                    ♡ 10
                    ◇ AQJ1043
                    ♣ AK54
```

At trick three, having taken the ♠AK, East led the ♣9, a deceptive card, though it wasn't quite clear whom it was intended to deceive.

South went up with the ♣A and drew trumps. Then he cashed the ♣K, just in case it brought down the ♣Q. When nothing happened, South played out his trumps, leaving himself with the ♡10 and the ♣54.

Discarding in front of dummy, West couldn't keep three hearts and the ♣Q. So he let go a heart and South brought in the ♡9 as his eleventh trick.

HAPPY ENDING

East knows from the bidding that South has at least ten cards in the minors. When he follows twice in spades, it is clear that he cannot have more than one heart. If it is the ♡Q, there is no hope. Similarly, if he has the three top clubs, he cannot be beaten.

If declarer is missing both the ♡Q and the ♣Q, he cannot make his contract—providing that, at trick three, East returns the ♡J, severing communications between declarer and his dummy, and so destroying the threat of a squeeze.

YOUR MOVE

Dealer South: Love All

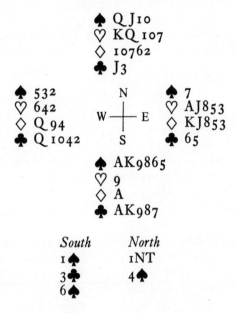

	South	North
	1♠	1NT
	3♣	4♠
	6♠	

CONTRACT 6♠ : LEAD ♠3

Declarer began by laying down the ♣A. His plan was to set up a long club by ruffing one in dummy.

This hand came up in a teams-of-four match. In one room the contract was made, in the other it went down.

No, this time you can't choose your seat. You are West. What happened?

THE AFTERMATH

In one room, declarer cashed his two top clubs and ruffed a club. Coming back to his hand with the ♢ A, he ruffed another club.

Next he ruffed a diamond to get back, drew two rounds of trumps and scored his fifth club for the twelfth trick. An easy hand.

HAPPY ENDING

In the other room, you sit West. Having listened carefully to the bidding, you realise the position. South must have eleven black cards. All his trumps are high and no one can prevent him, legitimately, from setting up his clubs.

Can he be dissuaded, perhaps, by some other means?

On the ♣A, you drop the ♣Q ! To all the world it looks like a singleton.

South hastily alters his plan to meet an unexpected situation. He draws trumps and runs the ♡ 9. If he finds you, West, with the ♡ J, he will discard two losing clubs on dummy's hearts. Unlucky. Not such an easy hand after all.

YOUR MOVE

Dealer East: N/S Vul:

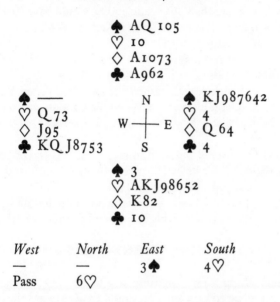

	♠ AQ 105	
	♡ 10	
	◇ A1073	
	♣ A962	

	West (♠ —)		East (♠ KJ987642)
	♡ Q 73	N	♡ 4
	◇ J95	W — E	◇ Q 64
	♣ KQ J8753	S	♣ 4

	♠ 3	
	♡ AKJ98652	
	◇ K82	
	♣ 10	

West	North	East	South
—	—	3♠	4♡
Pass	6♡		

CONTRACT 6♡ : LEAD ♣K

Will you run with the hare or hunt with the hounds? In other words, will you back South to make his contract or East-West to break it?

If you choose right, the story will have a happy ending.

THE AFTERMATH

South could play virtually double dummy. West could hardly have more than one spade and he would have surely led a singleton had he had one. Since he led the ♣K, he evidently had a void in spades.

Going up with the ♣A, South ruffed a club and continued with three rounds of trumps, losing to West's ♡Q. A club came back. South ruffed, cashed the ♠A and ruffed a spade. Then he reeled off his trumps. When the last one settled on the table, he had left ◇K42. In dummy were: ♠Q ♡– ◇A10 ♣9.

Having to discard before dummy, West was forced to part with a diamond, for he had to retain the ♣J. South could now throw dummy's ♣9 and turn the heat on East. To keep the best spade, he, too, had to let go a diamond. The double squeeze had materialised and South's ◇3 brought in the twelfth trick.

HAPPY ENDING

When, sitting West, you came in with the ♡Q, you realised what was going to happen. You would have to guard the clubs. Partner would have to keep the best spade. Who, then, would look after the diamonds?

To prevent the double squeeze from taking shape, you returned, not another club, but the ◇J. Now North-South communications were severed and the double squeeze was stillborn.

YOUR MOVE

Dealer South: Love All

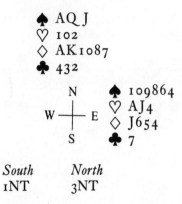

$$\begin{array}{l}
\spadesuit \text{ AQ J} \\
\heartsuit \text{ 102} \\
\diamondsuit \text{ AK1087} \\
\clubsuit \text{ 432}
\end{array}$$

	N	
W		E
	S	

$$\begin{array}{l}
\spadesuit \text{ 109864} \\
\heartsuit \text{ AJ4} \\
\diamondsuit \text{ J654} \\
\clubsuit \text{ 7}
\end{array}$$

South	*North*
1NT	3NT

CONTRACT 3NT: LEAD ♣Q

Declarer wins with the ♣A and continues with the ◇Q and ◇9 to dummy's ◇A. The ◇K and ◇10 follow, West discarding a small spade, then the ♣8.

What should East play when he comes in at trick five with the ◇J?

THE AFTERMATH

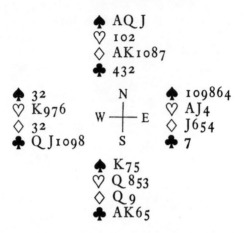

```
              ♠ A Q J
              ♡ 1 0 2
              ◇ A K 1 0 8 7
              ♣ 4 3 2

  ♠ 3 2              N              ♠ 1 0 9 8 6 4
  ♡ K 9 7 6      ──┼──              ♡ A J 4
  ◇ 3 2        W    E               ◇ J 6 5 4
  ♣ Q J 1 0 9 8      S              ♣ 7

              ♠ K 7 5
              ♡ Q 8 5 3
              ◇ Q 9
              ♣ A K 6 5
```

East led the ♡ A followed by the ♡ J. South covered and West made his ♡ K and ♡ 9, but the contract was unbreakable —on this defence.

HAPPY ENDING

Since West must have the ♡ K—and not the ♠ K—if the defence is to stand any chance at all, East does better to lead the ♡ J. Now he has an entry to lead through the closed hand a second time.

The ♡ J is covered by the ♡ Q and ♡ K. The ♡ 6 comes back, picking up dummy's ♡ 10. East wins with the ♡ A and leads the ♡ 4 through declarer's ♡ 85 up to West's ♡ 97.

East played well, but South shouldn't have given him the chance. Needing four diamonds only, and realising that hearts presented the only danger, he should have crossed to the ♠ A at trick two and led a low diamond, inserting the ◇ 9. Even if West made the bare ◇ J, the contract would be safe.

YOUR MOVE

Dealer South: N/S Vul:

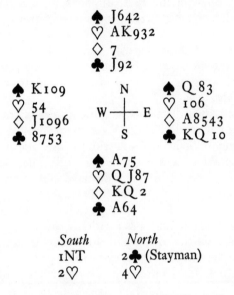

```
                    ♠ J642
                    ♡ AK932
                    ◇ 7
                    ♣ J92

   ♠ K109            N            ♠ Q83
   ♡ 54                           ♡ 106
   ◇ J1096      W ─┼─ E           ◇ A8543
   ♣ 8753            S            ♣ KQ10

                    ♠ A75
                    ♡ QJ87
                    ◇ KQ2
                    ♣ A64
```

South	*North*
1NT	2♣ (Stayman)
2♡	4♡

CONTRACT 4♡ : LEAD ◇J

Pick the winner.

Assuming the best dummy play and the best defence, will South make his contract?

THE AFTERMATH

East wins the first trick with the ◇ A and returns the ♣ K. South goes up with the ♣ A, draws trumps, parks two of dummy's clubs on his ◇ KQ and concedes two spades. No trouble.

We'll try again. East is a wily bird. He knows that South must have the ♣ A for his opening 1NT, so he plays low at trick one, hoping to exchange one diamond trick for two tricks in clubs.

South ruffs two diamonds in dummy, draws trumps and exits with a low spade. Should West go up with the ♠ K and switch to a club, South will win with the ♣ A and play a club back. After taking his second club, East will be end-played, faced with a choice of playing a diamond and so conceding a ruff and discard, or leading away from his ♠ Q.

Therefore, to foil South, West plays low to the first spade and East captures dummy's ♠ J with the ♠ Q. Then he leads the ♣ K. Should South win and throw East in again with a second club, he will have a safe exit with a spade.

Did you back the defence? No? You were quite right.

HAPPY ENDING

The play proceeds as before. South wins the first trick, ruffs his two remaining diamonds in dummy, draws trumps and exits with a low spade away from his ♠ A.

West plays low and dummy's ♠ J falls to East's ♠ Q. Once more, East leads the ♣ K, only this time South lets him hold the trick.

East cannot afford to lead a second club, for the ♣ J is still in dummy, while South retains the ♣ A. So he switches to a spade.

South goes up with his ♠ A and leads another spade. Now dummy's long spade takes care of a losing club, and declarer wins, after all.

YOUR MOVE

Dealer South: N/S Vul:

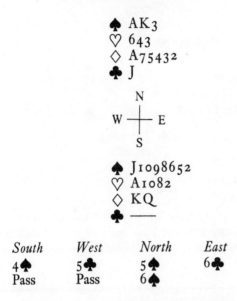

♠ AK3
♡ 643
◇ A75432
♣ J

```
        N
   W ——+—— E
        S
```

♠ J1098652
♡ A1082
◇ KQ
♣ —

South	West	North	East
4♠	5♣	5♠	6♣
Pass	Pass	6♠	

CONTRACT 6♠ : LEAD ♣K

With a void in clubs South made a forcing pass over East's
6♣, and bearing the vulnerability in mind, North was surely
right to bid the slam.

So long as neither defender had a void in spades or a singleton
diamond, declarer could see fourteen tricks. Meanwhile, he
set out to make twelve.

A 5-0 diamond break would be fatal but, that apart, he
wasn't worried. Ruffing the opening lead with the ♠2, he led
a trump to dummy's ♠K.

Do you agree?

THE AFTERMATH

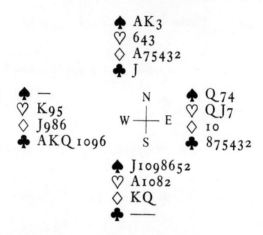

When West showed out on the first round of trumps, South switched to diamonds, but East declined to ruff and declarer couldn't set up the suit and ended losing two hearts, as well as a trump.

HAPPY ENDING

The correct play calls for a lot of forethought and few experts would find it at the table—except, of course, in the *post-mortem*. Declarer should ruff the first trick with the ♠ 5—or the ♠ J, for that matter—carefully preserving the ♠ 2. Next he should lay down the two top diamonds. If all follow, there's no problem. But East ruffs and returns a heart. South wins, takes out East's two remaining trumps with dummy's ♠ AK, and ruffs a diamond, setting up the suit.

All that remains is to get back to dummy by overtaking the ♠ 2 with the ♠ 3.

YOUR MOVE

Dealer North: Love All

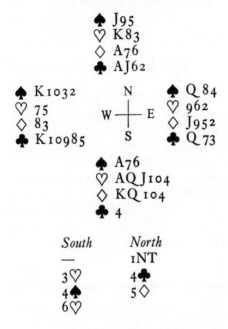

South	North
—	1NT
3♡	4♣
4♠	5♢
6♡	

CONTRACT 6♡ : LEAD ♡5

Declarer won in his hand and looked with understandable distaste at dummy's ugly shape. At trick two he led the ♠6, inserting the ♠9 from dummy.

East won the trick and returned another trump.

Who is going to win?

Place your bets, for at any moment the hand will come under starter's orders.

THE AFTERMATH

Winning in dummy, declarer led the ♣A and ruffed a club. Someone might have started with ♣KQ x. When nothing happened, he led the ♠A, but there were no miracles.

What could South do about his second spade loser?

HAPPY ENDING

One hope remained—that dummy's third spade could be discarded on declarer's fourth diamond. For that to be possible it was imperative that the diamonds should break 4–2— quite likely in itself—and that the defender who was short in diamonds should not have the last trump.

Hoping for the best, South laid down the ♢K and crossed to the ♢A—in case West had started with ♢Jx bare. Now he finessed the ♢10, and when West showed out and didn't ruff, all was well. South threw dummy's third spade on the ♢Q, ruffed a spade in dummy and claimed the contract.

YOUR MOVE

Dealer South: E/W Vul

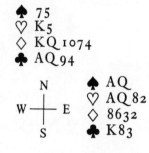

```
              ♠ 75
              ♡ K5
              ◇ KQ1074
              ♣ AQ94

         N            ♠ AQ
                      ♡ AQ82
    W ──┼── E         ◇ 8632
         S            ♣ K83
```

South
4♠   ALL PASS

CONTRACT 4♠ : LEAD ♡3

You sit East and the sight of dummy fills you with gloom. When *you* make bold, pre-emptive bids, partner puts down a collection of rubbish—enough to stop opponents getting anywhere, but with no possible trick for you.

Declarer plays dummy's ♡K and you win with the ♡A.

Without looking for miracles, how do you propose to defeat the contract?

THE AFTERMATH

```
                    ♠ 75
                    ♡ K5
                    ◇ KQ1074
                    ♣ AQ94

    ♠ 32              N              ♠ AQ
    ♡ J963                           ♡ AQ82
    ◇ J9        W ──┼── E            ◇ 8632
    ♣ J10652          S              ♣ K83

                    ♠ KJ109864
                    ♡ 1074
                    ◇ A3
                    ♣ 7
```

East cashed his ♡Q and continued with a low diamond. Declarer won in dummy and led a trump to East's ♠A.

Another diamond came back, but South was in no trouble. He won in his hand, drew trumps and spread his hand.

Had East led the ♠A, followed by the ♠Q, at trick three—or trick two—it would have done him no good. Trumps having been drawn for him, declarer would have run the diamonds or ruffed them out, had it been necessary, using the ♣A as an entry.

HAPPY ENDING

East can break the contract by playing the ♠Q at trick two.

The lead of the ♡3, East himself having the ♡2, indicates a four-card suit and an honour. So South has three hearts. If he had the ♡J, he wouldn't play dummy's king at trick one. It follows that South has three losing hearts and East must prevent him from ruffing one in dummy—without surrendering trump control.

If East leads the ♠Q at trick two, South is helpless. He can try the club finesse or take three rounds of diamonds to get rid of a heart, but West will ruff and that will be that.

YOUR MOVE

Dealer South: Love All

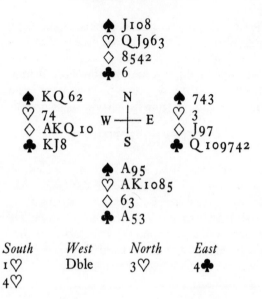

	♠ J108	
	♡ QJ963	
	◇ 8542	
	♣ 6	

♠ KQ62	N	♠ 743
♡ 74	W — E	♡ 3
◇ AKQ10	S	◇ J97
♣ KJ8		♣ Q109742

	♠ A95	
	♡ AK1085	
	◇ 63	
	♣ A53	

South	*West*	*North*	*East*
1♡	Dble	3♡	4♣
4♡			

CONTRACT 4♡ : LEAD ◇K

Pick the winners.

By all means, look carefully at all four hands, so long as you bear in mind that neither side could do so when this deal occurred in a teams-of-four match.

Well, will South make his contract?

THE AFTERMATH

In one room, West continued with the ◇ A and then the ◇ Q, which South ruffed.

On the face of it, the contract depended on finding the spade honours divided, but West's take-out double of 1 ♡ pretty well marked him with both, so South proceeded to eliminate. He ruffed two clubs in dummy and dummy's last diamond in his hand. Then he led the ♠ J, end-playing West, who had no choice but to lead away from his second spade honour.

HAPPY ENDING

In the other room, West looked ahead, He couldn't be sure that East had the ◇ J, but his second diamond trick couldn't run away, so, at trick two, he switched to a trump.

South still tried to eliminate, but to do so he had to play another diamond. East promptly went up with the ◇ J and shot a spade through the closed hand.

Now West could no longer be end-played.

YOUR MOVE

Dealer West: Both Vul:

```
              ♠ A K
              ♡ J 8 6 5 2
              ◇ A 9 6 4
              ♣ A K

                    N
              W  ──┼── E
                    S

              ♠ Q J 1 0 9 6
              ♡ —
              ◇ 7 5 3 2
              ♣ Q J 1 0 3
```

South	North
—	1 ♡
1 ♠	3 ◇
4 ◇	4 ♠

CONTRACT 4♠ : LEAD ♡K

Lesser players, well, much lesser, shall we say, might have found themselves in 3NT.

South heaved a sigh of relief when he saw dummy. With five trumps, four clubs and the ◇ A, he had ten top tricks.

In which order should he gather them?

THE AFTERMATH

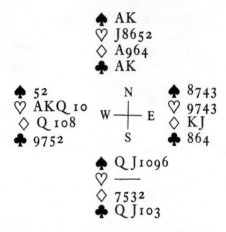

```
                    ♠ AK
                    ♡ J8652
                    ◇ A964
                    ♣ AK
    ♠ 52              N            ♠ 8743
    ♡ AKQ10                        ♡ 9743
    ◇ Q108      W ─┼─ E            ◇ KJ
    ♣ 9752             S           ♣ 864
                    ♠ QJ1096
                    ♡ ——
                    ◇ 7532
                    ♣ QJ103
```

Declarer ruffed the ♡ K, cashed the ♠ AK, then the ♣ AK and crossed to his hand with a heart ruff to draw trumps. He couldn't have got back any other way, but neither could he afford to force himself, for now trump control passed to East and the fourth club was brutally ruffed, and so, declarer's tenth trick never saw the light of day.

HAPPY ENDING

That good looking club suit was a snare and a delusion. Declarer couldn't enjoy it—but then he didn't need it in the first place. He had ten tricks without it with: five trumps in his own hand; two club ruffs in dummy; the ◇ A and the ♣ AK.

There was nothing unlucky about the 4–2 trump break, which was in accordance with the odds. Now had someone ruffed the ◇ A or the second club, that really would have been unlucky.

YOUR MOVE

Dealer South: E/W Vul:

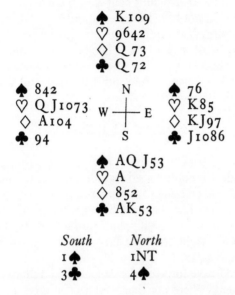

```
            ♠ K109
            ♡ 9642
            ◇ Q73
            ♣ Q72
♠ 842              N              ♠ 76
♡ QJ1073      W —┼— E            ♡ K85
◇ A104                           ◇ KJ97
♣ 94               S             ♣ J1086
            ♠ AQJ53
            ♡ A
            ◇ 852
            ♣ AK53
```

South	North
1♠	1NT
3♣	4♠

CONTRACT 4♠ : LEAD ♡Q

North's jump to 4♠ may seem bold, but though his points are few, he has two important cards. The ♣Q is obviously worth more than two points, just as the ♠K is worth more than three.

As dummy goes down, declarer can see nine top tricks, ten if the clubs break 3–3, though that is against the odds.

It is clearly hopeless to try for a trick in diamonds, for if West had the ◇AK, he would have surely led the suit.

What can South do to improve his chances?

THE AFTERMATH

South thought of taking two rounds of trumps and then
testing the clubs. If the clubs split 4–2, the defender with the
doubleton might not have the last trump.

If only dummy had another entry. . . .

Suddenly, South had an idea. The clubs, after all, wouldn't
run away. Meanwhile, given the chance, opponents might
provide a little assistance. So South led a diamond and boldly
went up with dummy's ◇Q.

HAPPY ENDING

East won the trick with the ◇K and obligingly returned a
heart. Now declarer didn't need that additional entry to dummy.

He ruffed, and crossing to dummy twice with trumps, ruffed
two more hearts. That brought his total to six tricks. Going
back to the table with the ♣Q, he drew the outstanding trump
with the ♠K—eight tricks so far—and scored the last two
tricks with the ♣AK.

East should have foreseen the dangers of a dummy reversal,
but that's neither here nor there. South conjured up an extra
chance out of the blue and brought home a contract on which
destiny doubtless intended him to go down.

YOUR MOVE

Dealer South: Love All

♠ 62
♡ 75
◇ Q 10752
♣ J975

N
W —— E
S

♠ AQ J9753
♡ K94
◇ A
♣ AK

South	North
2♣	2◇
2♠	3◇
3♠	3NT
4♠	

CONTRACT 4♠ : LEAD ◇6

East plays the ◇8 and as declarer gathers the first trick he begins to look for nine more.

He can see eight. What is his best chance of finding a ninth and which card should he play at trick two?

THE AFTERMATH

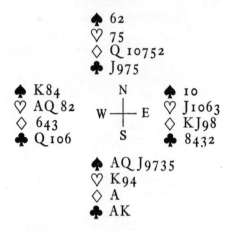

♠ 62
♡ 75
◇ Q 10752
♣ J975

♠ K84
♡ AQ 82
◇ 643
♣ Q 106

♠ 10
♡ J1063
◇ KJ98
♣ 8432

♠ AQ J9735
♡ K94
◇ A
♣ AK

South would have liked to take the trump finesse, but having no entry to dummy, he had to think of something better. So, at trick two, he led a heart, hoping that a heart ruff in dummy would yield him his tenth trick.

East won and returned the ♠ 10. South seized the chance to take the trump finesse, but when it failed, the contract failed with it, for West's trump return put an end to all hopes of a heart ruff in dummy.

HAPPY ENDING

A heart ruff is just about the only hope, short of finding a singleton ♠ K, but declarer greatly improves his chances by leading the ♡ K at trick two. Half the time West will have the ♡ A, and if either defender has the doubleton ♠ K, neither can afford to lead a trump.

As the cards lie, West wins with the ♡ A and leads a trump, but now, when East comes in with the next heart, he has no trump to play. If West wins, he cannot lead a second trump without giving up his ♠ K.

YOUR MOVE

Dealer South: N/S Vul:

```
                ♠ 6
                ♡ 962
                ◇ KQ 10543
                ♣ 863

                    N
              W ──┼── E
                    S

                ♠ A1053
                ♡ AK3
                ◇ 62
                ♣ AQ 42
```

South	North
1♣	1◇
2NT	3◇
3NT	

CONTRACT 3NT: LEAD ♠K

Clearly, South was one of those bidding acrobats who regards a sign off as encouraging. North had heard him bid 2NT and could have raised to 3NT without further ado. His 3◇ bid said plainly that he didn't think South could make even 2NT.

"Really?" said South, in effect, "Well, if you don't think much of 2NT, let's play in 3NT."

Would you expect a man who bids like that to play well? Of course not. So please take over the South hand.

After the ♠K comes the ♠Q. You play low both times and West switches to a heart.

Continue.

THE AFTERMATH

```
                    ♠ 6
                    ♡ 962
                    ◇ KQ 10543
                    ♣ 963
    ♠ KQJ94         N          ♠ 872
    ♡ 105                      ♡ QJ87
    ◇ J987      W ─┼─ E        ◇ A
    ♣ K10           S          ♣ J875
                    ♠ A1053
                    ♡ AK3
                    ◇ 62
                    ♣ AQ42
```

What the mental acrobat intended to do, before you took
over, was to finesse the ◇ 10 and hope for the best.

He would have been overjoyed, no doubt, to see East win
with the ◇ A, but his pleasure wouldn't have lasted long and
the unlucky 4–1 diamond break would have been his main
standby in the post-mortem.

HAPPY ENDING

Fortunately, you took over the South hand just in time.
Winning the third trick, a heart, you promptly played the ◇ 2
from your hand and the ◇ 3 from dummy!

No, you didn't see through the backs of the cards, but you
played for the only possible distribution to give you the contract.

Unless the ◇ A is bare, it will be held up, so no finesse can
help—on the first round. Neither would it be any good finding
the bare ◇ A with West, for then East stops the suit. Only as
the cards lie can the contract be made, for once East's ◇ A is
out of the way, West's ◇ J can be brought down after the
marked finesse.

YOUR MOVE

Dealer West: Love All

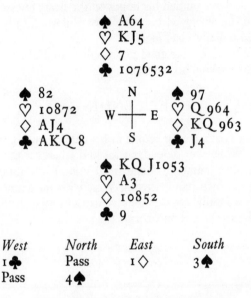

```
                  ♠ A64
                  ♡ KJ5
                  ◇ 7
                  ♣ 1076532
   ♠ 82              N        ♠ 97
   ♡ 10872                    ♡ Q964
   ◇ AJ4       W ─┼─ E        ◇ KQ963
   ♣ AKQ8          S          ♣ J4
                  ♠ KQJ1053
                  ♡ A3
                  ◇ 10852
                  ♣ 9
```

West	North	East	South
1♣	Pass	1◇	3♠
Pass	4♠		

CONTRACT 4♠: LEAD ♣K

At trick two West switched to a trump. Declarer won in dummy and led the ◇7. Going up with the ◇Q, East returned a second trump.

Only one trump now remained in dummy.

How should South play to make certain of his contract?

THE AFTERMATH

Since he could only ruff one diamond and couldn't afford to lose two, declarer pinned his hopes on the heart finesse. When that failed, he shrugged his shoulders philosophically. North murmured politely "bad luck".

Neither bad luck nor good philosophy should have stopped South from making his contract.

HAPPY ENDING

Winning East's trump return in his hand, South gives up a diamond. Whichever defender wins and whatever the return, declarer ruffs a diamond—his third diamond—in dummy and a club in his own hand, leaving West with no diamond and East with no club. Now it only remains to play trumps. As South reaches the last one, this is the position.

```
                    ♠ —
                    ♡ KJ5
                    ◇ —
                    ♣ 10

   ♠ —                   N                ♠ —
   ♡ 1087                                 ♡ Q96
   ◇ —          W ──┼── E                 ◇ K
   ♣ A                                    ♣ —
                    S

                    ♠ J
                    ♡ A3
                    ◇ 10
                    ♣ —
```

To keep his ♣A west has to part with a heart. Having served its purpose, dummy's ♣10 is now discarded and the heat is turned on East.

Since he must retain the ◇K he, too, lets go a heart.

The double squeeze has taken effect and the ♡Q—wherever she may be—dutifully comes down.

YOUR MOVE

Dealer South: Both Vul:

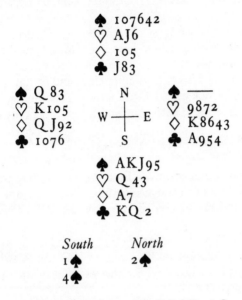

```
                    ♠ 107642
                    ♡ AJ6
                    ◇ 105
                    ♣ J83
        ♠ Q83            N            ♠ —
        ♡ K105                        ♡ 9872
        ◇ QJ92      W ─┼─ E          ◇ K8643
        ♣ 1076          S            ♣ A954
                    ♠ AKJ95
                    ♡ Q43
                    ◇ A7
                    ♣ KQ2
```

South	*North*
1♠	2♠
4♠	

CONTRACT 4♠: LEAD ◇Q

One look at dummy and South begins, mentally, to add up the score. His joy, however, will soon give way to gloom, for once East shows out in trumps, a fourth loser will appear upon the scene.

Surely there is now a loser in every suit.

How should South play to give himself the best chance?

THE AFTERMATH

South went up with the ♢ A and laid down the ♠ A. When East showed out, a seemingly cast-iron contract began to look shaky.

A throw-in against West offered the best chance, so South began by clearing his clubs. East won and returned the ♡ 9, taken by dummy's ♡ J.

Declarer cashed his two winning clubs and continued with a diamond. East took the trick and returned another heart.

Losing one trick in each suit, South had to concede defeat.

HAPPY ENDING

South shouldn't have given East-West the chance to defend so well. His idea of an end-play against West was sound enough and it would have succeeded—at trick one. After that, it was too late.

If West is allowed to hold the ♢ Q, communications between defenders are disrupted. East cannot lead hearts twice, and after cashing his clubs, declarer throws West in with a trump, leaving this position:

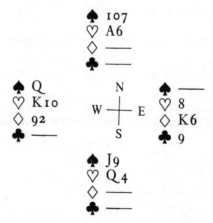

West must either lead a heart or present South with a ruff and discard.

YOUR MOVE

Dealer South: E/W Vul:

♠ 74
♡ 86
◇ 6532
♣ J9862

```
        N
   W  ──┼──  E
        S
```

♠ AKQ 2
♡ AK
◇ KQ J 10
♣ K54

South	*North*
2♣	2◇
3NT	

CONTRACT 3NT: LEAD ♡Q

When you pick up a really good hand, you find an utterly worthless dummy. It doesn't happen to other people—or at least it doesn't seem like it—but that is no consolation.

It wouldn't matter so much at duplicate, for then all the other Souths would be in the same boat. But this is rubber bridge and you are not likely to pick up a hand like that for months.

How do you play to give yourself the best chance?

THE AFTERMATH

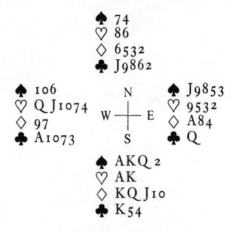

South cleared the diamonds, but he could take only eight tricks before defenders came in again.

His one feeble hope was that a defender with four spades would throw one on his fourth diamond. Declarer missed a far better chance.

HAPPY ENDING

At trick two, he should lead the ♣K—not because he has seen East's hand, but because it is the right play psychologically. If the ♣A and ♣Q are divided, the defender with the ♣A— especially West, sitting with Axx—is almost certain to hold it up. Not knowing the true position, his main concern will be to cut declarer's communications with his dummy.

Having scored his ninth trick, South can afford to attend to the other eight.

If the cards lie as in the diagram above, South takes ten tricks. That is, of course, purely incidental. What matters is that he would probably take nine, even if East had a second club.

YOUR MOVE

Dealer North: Love All

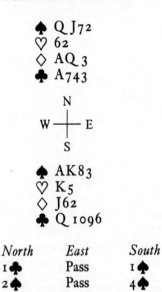

♠ Q J 7 2
♡ 6 2
◇ A Q 3
♣ A 7 4 3

N
W —— E
S

♠ A K 8 3
♡ K 5
◇ J 6 2
♣ Q 1 0 9 6

West	North	East	South
—	1♣	Pass	1♠
2♡	2♠	Pass	4♠

CONTRACT 4♠ : LEAD ♣8

Declarer can infer from the bidding that West has the ♡A and almost certainly the ◇K, as well.

How should he play?

THE AFTERMATH

```
                    ♠ Q J 7 2
                    ♡ 6 2
                    ◇ A Q 3
                    ♣ A 7 4 3
♠ 1 0 6 4              N              ♠ 9 5
♡ A Q J 7 4 3                        ♡ 1 0 9 8
◇ K 1 0 8     W ─┼─ E                ◇ 9 7 5 4
♣ 8                   S              ♣ K J 5 2
                    ♠ A K 8 3
                    ♡ K 5
                    ◇ J 6 2
                    ♣ Q 1 0 9 6
```

South ducked in dummy and East, winning with the ♣K, gave his partner a ruff. West exited safely with a trump, but now declarer drew two more rounds of trumps, finessed the ◇Q, cashed the ◇A and threw West in with the ◇K, forcing him to lead a heart up to South's ♡K. Only one down.

Declarer played well, but had he played better still, he would have made his contract.

HAPPY ENDING

The ♣8 is clearly "top of nothing" and may well be a singleton, as above. South goes up, therefore, with dummy's ♣A and—showing commendable foresight—unblocks, by throwing his ♣9.

Trumps are drawn, ending in dummy, and the ♣7 follows. East wins—or the lead would remain in dummy—and returns a heart which he is allowed to hold.

The defence is powerless. If a second heart follows, West is end-played. If East switches to a diamond, it doesn't help. Declarer wins with dummy's ◇Q, takes the finesse against East's ♣J, and throws West in with the ♡A, losing no diamond.

YOUR MOVE

Match-Pointed Pairs

Dealer South: Love All

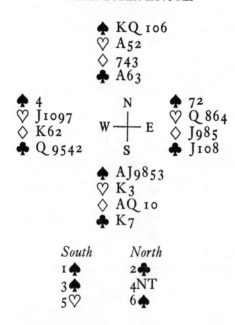

```
              ♠ KQ 106
              ♡ A52
              ◇ 743
              ♣ A63
♠ 4                          ♠ 72
♡ J1097          N           ♡ Q 864
◇ K62        W ─┼─ E         ◇ J985
♣ Q 9542         S           ♣ J108
              ♠ AJ9853
              ♡ K3
              ◇ AQ 10
              ♣ K7
```

South	*North*
1♠	2♣
3♠	4NT
5♡	6♠

CONTRACT 6♠ : LEAD ♡J

With so many top cards making up his 13 count, North felt too strong for a jump to 4♠. Playing limit raises, he was far too good for 3♠.

The answer was a delayed game raise. Had South's rebid been 2♡ or 2◇, a raise to 4♠ would now show values just insufficient for a forcing take-out.

Over the strong 3♠ rebid, North's course was clear.

On the face of it, the contract is unbeatable. Declarer strips the hand, leads a diamond, covers East's card and end-plays West.

Can you see any hope for the defence?

THE AFTERMATH

South drew trumps in two rounds, ruffed dummy's third heart and third club, and crossing to the table with a trump, led a diamond inserting the ◇ 10 from his hand.

This was the position:

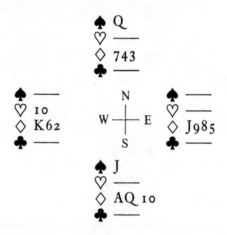

Without flinching, West followed with the ◇ 2.

HAPPY ENDING

South thought that he could now make all thirteen tricks. So he went back to dummy with the last trump, West calmly throwing the ◇ 6, and led another diamond, all set to go one down.

Alas, East followed unthinkingly with the ◇ 9. Since his last card couldn't be both the ◇ K and the ◇ J, South woke up to the position. West's good play cost him a cold bottom, while South scored a wholly undeserved top.

YOUR MOVE

Dealer East: N/S Vul:

```
            ♠ 63
            ♡ A62
            ◇ AQ 1063
            ♣ KQ 3

              N
         W ──┼── E
              S

            ♠ AQ
            ♡ K75
            ◇ J94
            ♣ J7652
```

West	North	East	South
—	—	1NT	Pass
		(12–14)	
2♠	Dble	3♠	3NT

CONTRACT 3NT: LEAD ♠J

You are South. Do you agree with your bidding or would you have been tempted to double 3♠?

No matter. If you make your contract, partner will forgive you. If you fail, he won't—and he will be right.

How do you play?

THE AFTERMATH

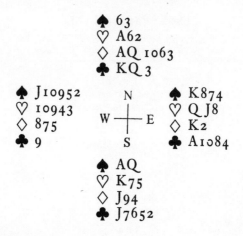

```
              ♠ 63
              ♡ A62
              ◇ AQ 1063
              ♣ KQ 3
♠ J10952         N        ♠ K874
♡ 10943                   ♡ Q J8
◇ 875       W ─┼─ E       ◇ K2
♣ 9              S        ♣ A1084
              ♠ AQ
              ♡ K75
              ◇ J94
              ♣ J7652
```

At trick two, declarer led a club to the king and ace. The spade return cleared the suit for the defence, and when the clubs didn't break and the diamond finesse failed, declarer had to concede defeat.

Unlucky?

HAPPY ENDING

Of course, that isn't how you played the hand. Placing East with both the ♣A and the ◇K on his opening bid, you entered dummy with the ◇A at trick two and led a low club. Had East gone up with the ♣A, you would have had nine tricks, so East played low.

With one club trick in the bag, you now had time to clear the diamonds, making: two spades, two hearts, four diamonds, and one club—the ninth trick.

YOUR MOVE

Dealer South: Love All

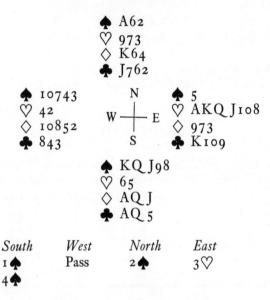

	♠ A62	
	♡ 973	
	◇ K64	
	♣ J762	

```
            N
♠ 10743          ♠ 5
♡ 42         W─┼─E    ♡ AKQJ108
◇ 10852          ◇ 973
♣ 843        S        ♣ K109

            ♠ KQJ98
            ♡ 65
            ◇ AQJ
            ♣ AQ5
```

South	West	North	East
1♠	Pass	2♠	3♡
4♠			

CONTRACT 4♠: LEAD ♡4

East won the first two tricks with the ♡AK and continued with the ♡Q.

Which card do you play?

Assuming that you ruff high and West discards a club, how do you continue?

THE AFTERMATH

Of course, declarer would have been wiser to discard a club at trick three. No doubt, he thought that he could make his contract even if West turned up with the ♣K.

The ♠K and ♠Q followed the heart ruff, and when East showed out, South gave up.

"I can't eat my loser", he said sorrowfully.

"Why not?" asked a kibitzer, and he was right, of course, as kibitzers always are.

HAPPY ENDING

The trump break is unfortunate, but all isn't lost. South cashes his three diamonds, ending in dummy, and successfully negotiates the club finesse. Next he cashes the ♣A. West has to follow all the way and this is the three-card end-position:

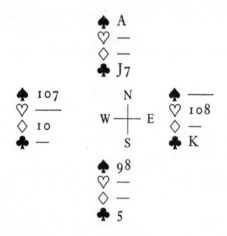

Declarer exits with the ♣5. It would do West no good to ruff, so he throws his ◇10. East wins and must, perforce, lead a heart.

West's trump winner—the one South couldn't eat—is smothered. If he over-ruffs declarer, the ♠A wins the trick. If West under-ruffs, the ♣J is thrown from dummy.

YOUR MOVE

Dealer West: Both Vul:

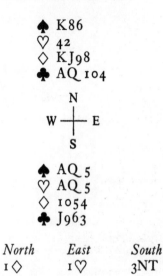

♠ K86
♡ 42
♢ KJ98
♣ AQ 104

```
        N
   W ──┼── E
        S
```

♠ AQ 5
♡ AQ 5
♢ 1054
♣ J963

West	North	East	South
Pass	1 ♢	1 ♡	3NT

CONTRACT 3NT: LEAD ♡8

This isn't a very different hand and the kibitzers will be entitled to raise their eyebrows if South goes down. Kibitzers, it is true, can gaze at all four hands, but declarer, too, should be able to see a little through the backs of the cards.

East plays the ♡ K and South wins.

Which card should South play at trick two?

THE AFTERMATH

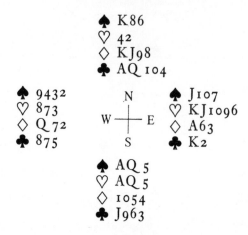

♠ K86
♡ 42
♢ KJ98
♣ AQ 104

♠ 9432   ♠ J107
♡ 873   ♡ KJ1096
♢ Q 72   ♢ A63
♣ 875   ♣ K2

♠ AQ 5
♡ AQ 5
♢ 1054
♣ J963

At trick two, South led the ♣9 and finessed. East won, cleared the hearts and scored three heart tricks, when he came in with the ♢ A. One down.

Declarer murmured something like "never known to bring off a finesse", which is what happens to players who take the wrong finesses.

HAPPY ENDING

It requires no crystal to give the diamond finesse preference over the finesse in clubs. On his vulnerable overcall East is pretty well marked with the ♢ A. If he has both the ♢ Q and the ♣ K as well, there's no hope. So long as one of these key cards is with West, all is well.

South should run the ♢ 10. If he loses to the ♢ Q, there is still time for the club finesse.

What if East, sitting with the ♢ AQ and no ♣ K, wins the first diamond with the ♢ A? He can count declarer's tricks and might try to deceive him.

If so, he will have found a brilliant defence and he will deserve to succeed. Just the same, South should run the ♢ 10, not the ♣ 9.

YOUR MOVE

Dealer South: N/S Vul:

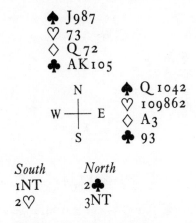

```
              ♠ J987
              ♡ 73
              ◇ Q72
              ♣ AK105
                           ♠ Q1042
              N            ♡ 109862
          W ──┼── E        ◇ A3
              S            ♣ 93
```

South	North
1NT	2♣
2♡	3NT

CONTRACT 3NT : LEAD ◇4

East wins with the ◇ A, declarer following with the ◇ 5.
What are the prospects for the defence and which card
should East lead at trick two?

THE AFTERMATH

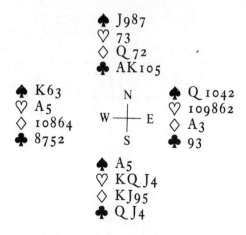

♠ J987
♡ 73
◇ Q 72
♣ AK105

♠ K63
♡ A5
◇ 10864
♣ 8752

N
W — E
S

♠ Q 1042
♡ 109862
◇ A3
♣ 93

♠ A5
♡ KQJ4
◇ KJ95
♣ QJ4

East returned the ◇ 3—he had been trained to play back partner's suit—and South had no trouble in collecting ten tricks.

HAPPY ENDING

As he gathers the first trick, East should have a pretty accurate picture of the deal. He can see the ◇ 2 and ◇ 3, so the lead of the ◇ 4 shows a four-card suit. That marks declarer with four diamonds, too. He bid 2♡ in response to North's 2♣ (Stayman), so he has four hearts.

Has he two clubs or three? If he had a doubleton, West would have five, and if so, he would have probably opened a club rather than a diamond.

That leaves South with two spades only. East should, therefore, switch at once to a spade. Unless declarer can reel off nine tricks, without losing the lead, he will surely go down. And if he can run nine tricks, the only effect of returning a diamond at trick two will be to give him a tenth.

YOUR MOVE

Dealer West: Both Vul:

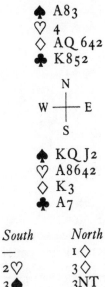

♠ A83
♡ 4
♢ AQ 642
♣ K852

```
        N
 W ──┼── E
        S
```

♠ KQJ2
♡ A8642
♢ K3
♣ A7

South	North
—	1♢
2♡	3♢
3♣	3NT
4♢	4♠
5♣	6♠

CONTRACT 6♠ : LEAD ♠4

Having limited his hand with two weak rebids, North could hold back no longer after South's cue bid in clubs.

When dummy went down, South was glad that he hadn't tamely passed 3NT. In a duplicate pairs event, he might have done. Fortunately, this was rubber bridge and the stakes were high.

What is the best line of play?

THE AFTERMATH

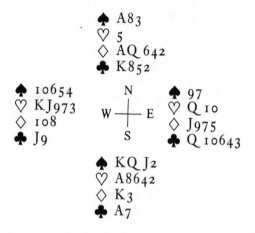

```
                    ♠ A 8 3
                    ♡ 5
                    ◇ A Q 6 4 2
                    ♣ K 8 5 2
    ♠ 10 6 5 4          N          ♠ 9 7
    ♡ K J 9 7 3     W ─┼─ E        ♡ Q 10
    ◇ 10 8             S           ◇ J 9 7 5
    ♣ J 9                          ♣ Q 10 6 4 3
                    ♠ K Q J 2
                    ♡ A 8 6 4 2
                    ◇ K 3
                    ♣ A 7
```

With ten top tricks, South decided to make two more by ruffing hearts in dummy. So he won the first trick with the ♠ A, played the ♡ A, ruffed a heart, came back to his hand with a club and ruffed another heart. When East over-ruffed, the only hope was a 3–3 diamond break. When that, too, failed to materialise, South regretted that he hadn't stayed in 3NT after all.

HAPPY ENDING

Declarer was unlucky to be over-ruffed in hearts, but the 4–2 breaks in trumps and in diamonds were to be expected. He could have allowed for them, however, by the simple expedient of playing a low diamond from both hands at trick two.

Winning the trump return—the defence can do no better—South lays down the ♡ A, ruffs a heart, comes to hand with the ♣ A and draws trumps. Now the ◇ K is cashed and the ♣ K is still in dummy as an entry to the ◇ A Q 6.

YOUR MOVE

Dealer South: N/S Vul:

♠ 105
♡ A853
◇ J753
♣ K94

```
        N
    W ──┼── E
        S
```

♠ AK8763
♡ K
◇ K82
♣ AQ5

South	North
1♠	1NT
4♠	

CONTRACT 4♠ : LEAD ♡Q

At trick two, South laid down the ♠A. West's card was the ♠Q and East's the ♠2.
How should declarer continue?

THE AFTERMATH

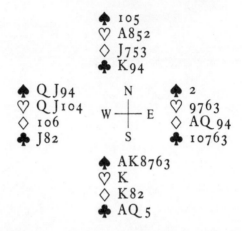

♠ 105
♡ A852
◇ J753
♣ K94

♠ Q J94   N   ♠ 2
♡ Q J104   W ─┼─ E   ♡ 9763
◇ 106   ◇ AQ 94
♣ J82   S   ♣ 10763

♠ AK8763
♡ K
◇ K82
♣ AQ 5

South crossed to dummy with a club, threw a diamond on the ♡ A and continued with the ♠ 10, intending to run it unless East covered.

Hoping to ensure against the loss of two trump tricks, declarer could afford to lose two diamonds.

When East showed out on the second spade, South realised that he would have the worst of both worlds, trumps and diamonds.

HAPPY ENDING

West found a brilliant defence, but South shouldn't have been taken in.

Finding the ◇ A with East, where he wanted it, was a straightforward fifty per cent chance. A singleton ♠ Q with West was no more than a three per cent chance.

South should have used his only entry to dummy to better purpose.

YOUR MOVE

Match-Pointed Pairs

Dealer South: Both Vul:

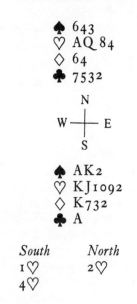

♠ 643
♡ AQ84
◇ 64
♣ 7532

```
        N
   W ——+—— E
        S
```

♠ AK2
♡ KJ1092
◇ K732
♣ A

South	*North*
1♡	2♡
4♡	

CONTRACT 4♡: LEAD ♣Q

At rubber bridge or in a teams-of-four match, the hand would play itself. Since West didn't open a trump, declarer would always have ten tricks with: two spades, five hearts, the ♣A and two diamond ruffs in dummy.

But this was a pairs event. The whole room would be in 4♡ and a mere ten tricks might result in a poor score.

How should South play?

THE AFTERMATH

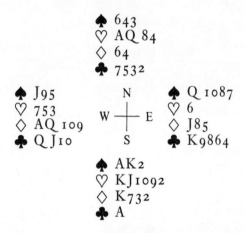

♠ 643
♥ AQ 84
◇ 64
♣ 7532

♠ J95   N   ♠ Q 1087
♥ 753   W —— E   ♥ 6
◇ AQ 109   ◇ J85
♣ Q J10   S   ♣ K9864

♠ AK2
♥ KJ1092
◇ K732
♣ A

It was no good being satisfied with ten tricks if other Souths made more, so at trick two declarer crossed to the ♥ A and led a diamond to his ◇ K. West won and returned a trump. Coming in again with a diamond, at trick four, West played his third trump, leaving one trump only in dummy to deal with two losing diamonds. One down.

HAPPY ENDING

South sacrifices nothing by leading a low diamond from his hand at trick two. He wins the trump return in dummy and now leads a diamond up to his ◇ K. If East has the ◇ A, dummy's third spade will be thrown on the ◇ K. South will still come to eleven tricks, but this way, no matter how the trumps and diamonds are divided, he will make his contract.

YOUR MOVE

Dealer South: Love All

♠ 62
♡ A103
◇ AJ932
♣ Q 62

```
        N
  W  ──┼──  E
        S
```

♠ AK
♡ Q 752
◇ 754
♣ AKJ3

South	North
1♣	1◇
2NT	3NT

CONTRACT 3NT: LEAD ♠J

Which card should declarer lead at trick two and what should be his plan of action?

THE AFTERMATH

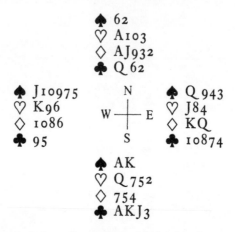

♠ 62
♡ A103
◇ AJ932
♣ Q 62

♠ J10975
♡ K96
◇ 1086
♣ 95

♠ Q 943
♡ J84
◇ KQ
♣ 10874

♠ AK
♡ Q 752
◇ 754
♣ AKJ3

South crossed to the ♣Q and led a low heart to his ♡Q. Half the time he would find East with the ♡K and he would be home, high and dry.

This, however, was the other half. West won the trick and drove out declarer's second spade stopper. Taking the finesse against the ♡J, South had a second even money chance, but when that, too, failed he bowed to an unkind fate.

HAPPY ENDING

South had given himself a seventy-five per cent chance, but he could have done even better. Since he wanted to lead a heart from dummy anyway, he should have crossed to the ◇A, not to the ♣Q. It couldn't cost anything and it might yield an extra chance. Seeing East drop the ◇K (or ◇Q), South would get back to his hand, finesse against West's ◇10 and land the contract without touching hearts.

What if East, sitting with the ♡K and the ◇KQ10, false cards? Won't a perfectly good contract vanish into the cold night air?

True. It will be a well-earned success for clever defence, but for all that declarer improves his chances by going to dummy with a diamond. The club can't help, the diamond may.

YOUR MOVE

Dealer West: Love All

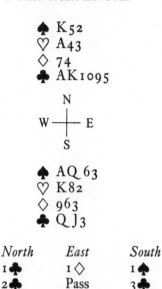

♠ K52
♡ A43
◇ 74
♣ AK1095

```
        N
  W ——+—— E
        S
```

♠ AQ63
♡ K82
◇ 963
♣ QJ3

West	North	East	South
Pass	1♣	1◇	1♠
Pass	2♣	Pass	3♣
Pass	3♠	Pass	4♠

CONTRACT 4♠ : LEAD ◇2

East won the first trick with the ◇ K and returned the ♡ Q.

This is a perfectly straightforward hand and there is nothing diabolical about the distribution.

How should declarer set about making his contract?

THE AFTERMATH

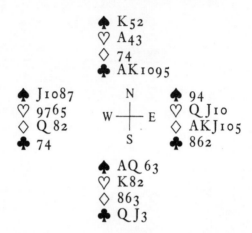

```
                    ♠ K52
                    ♡ A43
                    ◇ 74
                    ♣ AK1095
    ♠ J1087          N           ♠ 94
    ♡ 9765      W ──┼── E        ♡ QJ10
    ◇ Q 82           S           ◇ AKJ105
    ♣ 74                         ♣ 862
                    ♠ AQ 63
                    ♡ K82
                    ◇ 863
                    ♣ QJ3
```

Winning trick two with the ♡A, declarer led dummy's second diamond. East went up with the ◇A and drove out South's ♡K.

Declarer now ruffed a diamond, as planned, and turned his attention to trumps. The 4–2 break was disappointing, but not necessarily fatal. All would still be well if West followed to the third club. He would ruff the next one, but South would have his ten tricks with: four trumps, two hearts, a diamond ruff and three clubs.

West, alas, ruffed the third club and the heart return put paid to the contract.

HAPPY ENDING

The lure of the diamond ruff proved too much. Declarer doesn't need it and can't afford it.

At trick three he should play the ♠2 from dummy and the ♠3 from his hand. Now he is in full control. Whatever defenders play, he wins, draws trumps and enjoys five good clubs.

YOUR MOVE

Dealer South: Both Vul:

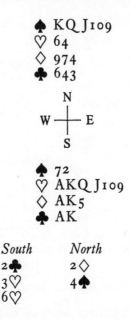

♠ KQJ109
♡ 64
◇ 974
♣ 643

♠ 72
♡ AKQJ109
◇ AK5
♣ AK

South	North
2♣	2◇
3♡	4♠
6♡	

CONTRACT 6♡ : LEAD ♣Q

The bidding has little to commend it, so South must make up for it by good play.

Prospects are admittedly poor, but can South, with a little luck and a little inspiration, conjure up a chance where none seems to exist?

No, neither defender has the singleton ♠A.

THE AFTERMATH

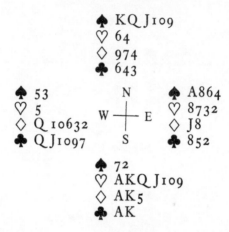

♠ KQJ109
♥ 64
♦ 974
♣ 643

♠ 53
♥ 5
♦ Q 10632
♣ QJ1097

♠ A864
♥ 8732
♦ J8
♣ 852

♠ 72
♥ AKQJ109
♦ AK5
♣ AK

South drew trumps in four rounds and led a spade. West signalled his doubleton and East held off. South wriggled for a while, but soon gave up.

HAPPY ENDING

Declarer shouldn't have surrendered so tamely. Envisaging a distribution such as the above, he cashes his second club before leading a spade. When he is on the table—East, of course, holds off—he ruffs dummy's third club.

Now comes the key play. South cashes his ♦ AK and exits with a spade. Having only spades left, East is powerless.

YOUR MOVE

Dealer South: Love All

      ♠ K 5
      ♡ 9643
      ◇ A8532
      ♣ K 7

            N
      W —┼— E
            S

      ♠ Q 82
      ♡ AK
      ◇ K6
      ♣ AJ6432

South	*North*
1♣	1◇
2NT	3NT

CONTRACT 3NT: LEAD ♠6

Declarer goes up with dummy's ♠ K which holds the trick.
What is the best line of play?

THE AFTERMATH

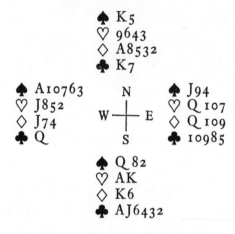

```
                    ♠ K 5
                    ♡ 9643
                    ◇ A8532
                    ♣ K 7
   ♠ A 10763          N          ♠ J 94
   ♡ J852                        ♡ Q 107
   ◇ J74       W ──┼── E         ◇ Q 109
   ♣ Q             S             ♣ 10985
                    ♠ Q 82
                    ♡ AK
                    ◇ K 6
                    ♣ AJ6432
```

Declarer's prime concern was to prevent East from gaining
the lead. So he laid down the ♣ K, intending to finesse against
East. When the ♣ Q came down, the sky quickly clouded over
and there was no silver lining. South had eight tricks and no
more. To set up the ninth he had to let East in with the ♣ 10 and
the spade return soon sealed his fate.

HAPPY ENDING

This hand belongs to the Department of Extra Chances.
South's plan is sound. It's his first move that's wrong. He
should come to his hand with the ◇ K and lead a club up to
dummy. When West produces the ♣ Q, he is allowed to hold
the trick. Now five clubs can be brought in, East is kept out and
all is well.

Is it very unlikely that the clubs should be divided in just
that way? Yes, but it is also unlikely for zero to come up at
roulette, yet casinos make a fortune out of that one slender
three per cent chance.

Playing the first club from the closed hand costs nothing and
once in a while, as on this occasion, it will hit the jackpot.

YOUR MOVE

Dealer South: N/S Vul:

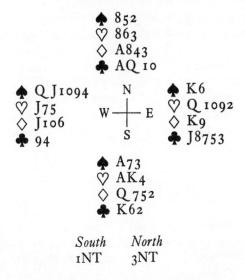

	South	North
	1NT	3NT

CONTRACT 3NT: LEAD ♠Q

East overtook with his ♠K, which was allowed to hold, and returned the ♠6.

Declarer held up his ♠A till the third round—on which East discarded thd ♣3—and continued with a diamond to dummy's ◇A, then a second diamond to East's ◇K.

Would you have played and defended the same way?

THE AFTERMATH

Since West had no entry, declarer remained in full control and brought home his contract with ease.

An elderly kibitzer shook his head in disapproval.

"You gave East two chances of beating you" he told South. "There was no need to hold up the ♠ A twice, for if East had a third spade the suit wasn't dangerous. Had East been awake, he would have taken the opportunity to jettison his ◇ K. He had a second chance to get rid of it on the ◇ A and either way you would have gone down.

"To prevent East from unblocking you should have crossed to the ♣ A and led a low diamond, away from the ◇ A. Then . . ."

HAPPY ENDING

"Then" broke in a second kibitzer "East plays the ◇ 9. South goes up, of course, with, his ◇ Q—for East must have the ◇ K or there's no hope—and continues with a second diamond. West plays the ◇ J and South must guess. If East started with a doubleton ◇ K, he must duck. If East has a third diamond, the ◇ 10 to be precise, South must go up with the ◇ A.

"It's a happy ending, for all concerned will have played well. As it was . . ."

YOUR MOVE

Dealer West: Game All

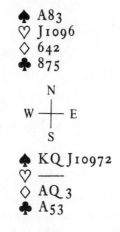

♠ A83
♡ J1096
◇ 642
♣ 875

```
        N
   W ——+—— E
        S
```

♠ KQJ10972
♡ ——
◇ AQ3
♣ A53

West	North	East	South
West	*North*	*East*	*South*
1♡	Pass	2♡	4♠

CONTRACT 4♠: LEAD ♡K

South has nine top tricks, but it doesn't look, on the bidding, as if the diamond finesse is likely to succeed.

What is the best line of play?

THE AFTERMATH

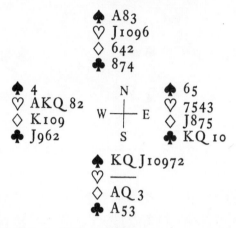

```
                    ♠ A83
                    ♡ J1096
                    ◇ 642
                    ♣ 874
♠ 4                      N              ♠ 65
♡ AKQ82                                 ♡ 7543
◇ K109         W ──┼── E                ◇ J875
♣ J962                   S              ♣ KQ10
                    ♠ KQJ10972
                    ♡ ──
                    ◇ AQ3
                    ♣ A53
```

South ruffed the ♡K and led out six more trumps to exert pressure on West, and he watched the discards like a hawk.

West parted with three clubs and two hearts, so South continued with a low club. Guessing, correctly, that West had left himself with a singleton honour, South hoped that he would be end-played. After taking two hearts he would have to lead a diamond. That was the plan.

East, however, overtook West's ♣J and shot through the ◇J. Down one.

HAPPY ENDING

South's plan might have worked, but he could have devised a better one.

He ruffs the ♡K with the ♠9—carefully preserving the ♠2—and goes over to dummy by overtaking the ♠K with the ♠A. At trick three he leads the ♡J, discarding a club. West wins and does best to return a club. South takes the ♣A, crosses to dummy by overtaking the ♠7 with the ♠8 and leads the ♡10, discarding another club.

West can only return a club, but South ruffs high and continues with that precious ♠2 to dummy's ♠3. The ♡9 scores the tenth trick.

YOUR MOVE

Dealer South: Love All

    ♠ J1093
    ♡ A852
    ◇ 72
    ♣ 964

    ♠ AK852
    ♡ K73
    ◇ AKQJ
    ♣ A

South	North
2♣	2◇
2♠	3♠
4◇	4♡
4NT	5◇
6♠	

CONTRACT 6♠ : LEAD ♣Q

South could have bid the slam directly over North's cue-bid of 4♡, but it cost nothing to apply Blackwood and it ensured that there was no misunderstanding.

It doesn't look like being a difficult contract. How should declarer set about making it?

THE AFTERMATH

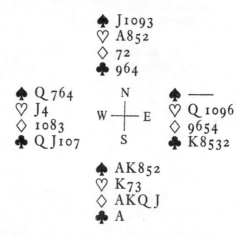

```
              ♠ J1093
              ♡ A852
              ◇ 72
              ♣ 964

♠ Q764         N          ♠ —
♡ J4       W ──┼── E      ♡ Q1096
◇ 1083         S          ◇ 9654
♣ QJ107                   ♣ K8532

              ♠ AK852
              ♡ K73
              ◇ AKQJ
              ♣ A
```

If the trumps broke 2-2 or if the ♠Q came down, South could count thirteen tricks. So, at trick two, he laid down the ♠A. When East showed out, he looked in the usual places for inspiration, but it was too late. The ceiling couldn't help.

South continued with a low trump. West went up with the ♠Q and returned another trump. That was good defence. Had West played a club, declarer would have gained a tempo and made his contract on a dummy reversal.

South's sole remaining hope was to find West with four diamonds, allowing him to discard two hearts from dummy. When that didn't materialise, there was nothing more he could do.

HAPPY ENDING

It isn't an easy play to find, but South can ensure his contract by leading the ♠8 at trick two. Regardless of what West does, there will now be two trump entries in dummy, enabling declarer to ruff two clubs in the closed hand.

Must it be the ♠8? Yes—in case East has all four trumps. It is by no means self-evident but, if you go through the motions, you will see that South cannot afford to play the ♠9 from dummy on the first round of trumps.

YOUR MOVE

Dealer West: Both Vul:

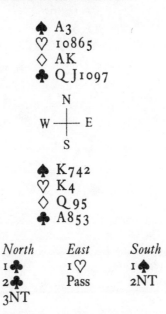

♠ A3
♡ 10865
◇ AK
♣ Q J1097

```
        N
   W ──┼── E
        S
```

♠ K742
♡ K4
◇ Q95
♣ A853

West	North	East	South
Pass	1♣	1♡	1♠
Pass	2♣	Pass	2NT
Pass	3NT		

CONTRACT 3NT: LEAD ♡Q

On the face of it, 5♣ looks an even better contract, and after East's vulnerable overcall, even a slam isn't unreasonable. Minor suit games, however, are always hard to reach and the lure of notrumps as an alternative is usually irresistible.

To the first trick, East follows with the ♡7.

How should declarer set about making his contract?

THE AFTERMATH

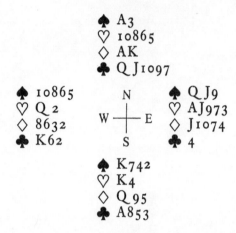

♠ A3
♡ 10865
♢ AK
♣ Q J1097

♠ 10865   N   ♠ Q J9
♡ Q 2   ♡ AJ973
♢ 8632   W —— E   ♢ J1074
♣ K62   S   ♣ 4

♠ K742
♡ K4
♢ Q 95
♣ A853

South won the first trick with the ♡ K, crossed to dummy's ♢ A and took the club finesse. Surely, on his vulnerable overcall, East should have had the ♣ K. That is true, and East would have been the first to admit it. West, however, won the trick and a second heart through dummy brought about South's undoing.

HAPPY ENDING

There was no need for South to be so unlucky. It is quite clear that West's ♡ Q is a singleton or doubleton. From ♡ Q xx —assuming that East had overcalled on a four-card suit— West would have led a low one. Declarer allows the ♡ Q to hold and is safe for ever after.

Yes, the ♡ K drops on the ♡ A, which is a little undignified, perhaps, but the ♡ 10 in dummy stops the suit and now declarer can take the club finesse without running the slightest risk.

YOUR MOVE

Dealer East: Love All

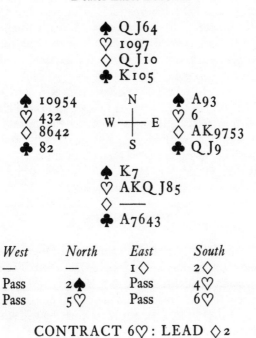

		♠ QJ64
		♡ 1097
		◇ QJ10
		♣ K105

♠ 10954   ♠ A93
♡ 432   ♡ 6
◇ 8642   ◇ AK9753
♣ 82   ♣ QJ9

♠ K7
♡ AKQJ85
◇ ——
♣ A7643

West	North	East	South
—	—	1◇	2◇
Pass	2♠	Pass	4♡
Pass	5♡	Pass	6♡

CONTRACT 6♡ : LEAD ◇2

Do you expect declarer to make his contract or do you fancy the chances of the defence?

Pick the winner.

THE AFTERMATH

At trick one declarer ruffed East's ◇ K, crossed to dummy with a trump and led a low spade. East ducked and the ♠ K won. South proceeded to draw trumps, ending in dummy. and ran the ◇ Q , discarding his ♠ 7. Had East covered, the result would have been the same, of course, for the ♣ K would have ensured an entry to the ◇ J.

Neither does it help East to go up with the ♠ A at trick three. Now a diamond trick is set up, as before, and three clubs are parked on dummy's winners in spades and diamonds.

If East plays low on the first spade, he loses his ♠ A. If he goes up with the ♠ A, he makes no trick in clubs.

For all that, looking far ahead, you doubtless picked East as the winner and so for you the story has a . . .

HAPPY ENDING

At trick one East plays low on the ◇ Q ! Declarer scores a wholly unexpected trick, but it does him no good. The discard comes too early. If he throws the ♠ 7, his ♠ K will drop on the ♠ A and he will have only two good spades in dummy to look after three losing clubs. If he throws a club, he will still lose a club and a spade.

YOUR MOVE

Dealer West: Love All

```
            ♠ K642
            ♡ AKQ
            ◇ AQ
            ♣ A753
              N
         W ——+—— E
              S
            ♠ A83
            ♡ J10983
            ◇ 753
            ♣ 94
```

West	North	East	South
Pass	2NT	Pass	3♡
Pass	4♣	Pass	4♡

CONTRACT 4♡ : LEAD ♡6

With a maximum and a superb fit in hearts, North had something to spare for his slam try, but when South signed off by rebidding his suit, he had to be satisfied with a game. Enough is enough.

In which order should declarer take his tricks?

THE AFTERMATH

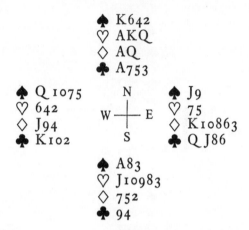

South could see nine top tricks and either the diamond finesse or a 3–3 spade break would yield the tenth. If both came off, he would score eleven and, but for difficulties in communications, he might, theoretically, come to twelve.

South began by testing the diamond position. He crossed to the closed hand with the ♠ A and took the losing finesse in diamonds. A second trump came back, leaving only one in dummy.

Declarer cashed his ♠ K, and played another, but the suit broke 4–2 and West, winning the third spade, promptly knocked out dummy's last trump. A crestfallen South conceded defeat.

HAPPY ENDING

Declarer's misfortune was dummy's seductive ◇ Q. Substitute a low diamond in her place, and all is well. Now there is no question of a finesse, so South doesn't waste the only entry to the closed hand to take it.

Finding himself in dummy at trick one, he cashes the ◇ A and leads the low one. A diamond ruff, which he takes when he comes in with the ♠ A, provides the tenth trick.

What a pity dummy wasn't just a little weaker.

YOUR MOVE

Dealer South: Both Vul:

♠ 8532
♡ Q 5
◇ K62
♣ Q J107

```
        N
  W ──┼── E
        S
```

♠ A74
♡ AKJ
◇ AQ 105
♣ AK3

South	North
2♣	2◇
3NT	6NT

CONTRACT 6NT: LEAD ♠K

North was an old-fashioned player or he would have responded not 2◇, but 2NT, to show a balanced hand with 7–9 scattered points. There was nothing wrong with the final contract, however—so long as South made it.

On the ♠ K East played the ♣ 6. South won and reeled off seven winners in clubs and hearts. On the fourth club West threw a spade and East a heart. Next came the ◇ A, the ◇ 5 to dummy's ◇ K—West following with the ◇ 4 and ◇ 8—and then dummy's third diamond. East's card was the ◇ 9.

Should South have made the contract for certain or did it depend on a guess in diamonds?

THE AFTERMATH

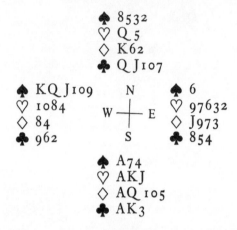

```
                    ♠ 8532
                    ♡ Q 5
                    ◊ K62
                    ♣ Q J107

  ♠ KQ J109      N        ♠ 6
  ♡ 1084     W ─┼─ E      ♡ 97632
  ◊ 84                    ◊ J973
  ♣ 962          S        ♣ 854

                    ♠ A74
                    ♡ AKJ
                    ◊ AQ 105
                    ♣ AK3
```

South misguessed and went down. He couldn't be sure of the position, for there was nothing to stop West from having four spades and three diamonds. And yet South should have made the contract without resorting to guesswork.

HAPPY ENDING

South went wrong in the usual place, trick one. He had nothing to gain by taking the ♠ K. Had he allowed it to hold, he would have discovered that West had five spades. Finding, later, that West had six cards in hearts and clubs he would have known that he couldn't have a third diamond.

If West followed three times in clubs, but twice only in hearts, the 3–3 diamond split would be a certainty. And if West turned up with only four cards in hearts and clubs, he would have been squeezed automatically, in diamonds and spades.

Had declarer paused a moment longer, at trick one . . .

YOUR MOVE

Dealer South: Love All

    ♠ A7
    ♡ A52
    ◇ AK8543
    ♣ A5

```
        N
   W ---+--- E
        S
```

    ♠ Q9653
    ♡ K8
    ♡ K8
    ◇ 6
    ♣ KQJ73

South	North
1♣	2◇
2♠	3◇
3♠	6♣

CONTRACT 6♣: LEAD ♡J

It must have given North a thrill to hear South open the bidding. How galling afterwards to stop short of a grand slam.

But what more could North do with a partner who had at least ten or eleven black cards? A bird in the hand . . .

South's problem was to make quite sure that the bird wouldn't fly away. How could he best sprinkle a little salt on its tail?

THE AFTERMATH

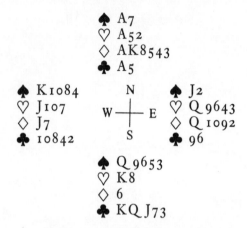

♠ A7
♡ A52
◇ AK8543
♣ A5

♠ K1084   N   ♠ J2
♡ J107   W ─┼─ E   ♡ Q9643
◇ J7   ◇ Q1092
♣ 10842   S   ♣ 96

♠ Q9653
♡ K8
◇ 6
♣ KQJ73

Declarer won the heart lead in his hand and drew trumps. In view of the 4–2 break he now needed the diamonds to be divided 3–3, and when that didn't materialise, he wished that he hadn't opened the bidding. Meanwhile, he consoled himself with the reflection that, had he played for a kindly spade break, he would have been no better off.

HAPPY ENDING

South could have coped with the 4–2 break in both minors either before or after drawing trumps. The most elegant solution of his problem is to lead the ◇ 6 at trick two and duck in dummy. He wins the heart return with the ♡ A, ruffs a diamond, draws trumps, and going over to the ♠ A, claims the rest.

Declarer can draw trumps first, but it looks prettier to duck the diamond at trick one.

YOUR MOVE

Dealer North: Love All

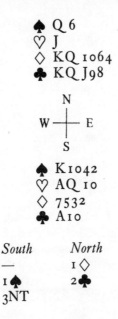

♠ Q 6
♡ J
♢ K Q 10 6 4
♣ K Q J 9 8

```
        N
  W  ──┼── E
        S
```

♠ K 10 4 2
♡ A Q 10
♢ 7 5 3 2
♣ A 10

South	North
—	1 ♢
1 ♠	2 ♣
3NT	

CONTRACT 3NT: LEAD ♡5

East played the ♡4 on dummy's ♡J and declarer could see a lot of tricks. Was there any danger? What if every card were wrong? Would it still be possible to make the contract?

What do you play at trick two?

THE AFTERMATH

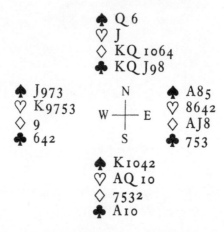

```
              ♠ Q 6
              ♡ J
              ◇ KQ 1064
              ♣ KQ J98
♠ J973          N          ♠ A85
♡ K9753                    ♡ 8642
◇ 9        W —┼— E         ◇ AJ8
♣ 642           S          ♣ 753
              ♠ K1042
              ♡ AQ 10
              ◇ 7532
              ♣ A10
```

Declarer overtook dummy's ♡J with his ♡Q to lead diamonds, up to dummy. East went up with the ◇A and returned a heart. With the ◇J wrong as well, declarer could do no better than take eight tricks.

HAPPY ENDING

The three cards that mattered—the ♡K, the ◇A and the ◇J—all were wrong, but declarer should have made his contract just the same.

Winning the first trick in dummy, he leads the ♠6. If East goes up with the ♠A, South has nine tricks. If East plays low, South takes the ♠K and sets up a diamond for his ninth trick.

Should West turn up with the ♠A, he cannot lead another heart. At worst, the defence will score three tricks in spades and the ◇A.

YOUR MOVE

Dealer South: Love All

```
        ♠ 832
        ♡ 752
        ◇ AK3
        ♣ AK103

            N
        W ──┼── E
            S

        ♠ K54
        ♡ AKJ64
        ◇ 95
        ♣ QJ6
```

South	North
1♡	2♣
2♡	4♡

CONTRACT 4♡ : LEAD ◇Q

With a combined count of 28, a five-card suit and a reasonable fit in trumps, the contract should be in the bag. And yet it could slip out. Bags aren't always watertight and this one is no exception.

How should declarer play to avoid losing three spades and a heart?

THE AFTERMATH

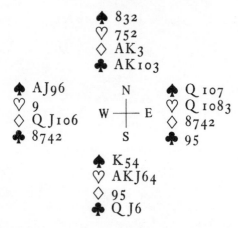

```
                ♠ 832
                ♡ 752
                ♢ AK3
                ♣ AK103
♠ AJ96         N          ♠ Q107
♡ 9                       ♡ Q1083
♢ QJ106    W ─┼─ E        ♢ 8742
♣ 8742         S          ♣ 95
                ♠ K54
                ♡ AKJ64
                ♢ 95
                ♣ QJ6
```

South's main concern was to keep East out, so as to avoid a hostile spade switch before the trumps were cleared. At trick two he led the ♡2. East followed with the ♡3 and declarer's ♡J won. All was set fair for the next couple of seconds. Then West showed out on the ♡A and there was no longer any hope of keeping East out of the lead.

Declarer cashed the ♡K and turned to the clubs. If East followed three times, the long club would take care of a spade. East could ruff, of course, but it would be with a winning trump.

Unfortunately for South, East had two clubs only. He ruffed the third club, and with the ♠A offside, there was no way of avoiding three more losers.

HAPPY ENDING

The 4–1 trump break was unkind, but South could have guarded against it at trick two by inserting the ♡4 on East's ♡3. Unless West had a void, he couldn't help overtaking the trick. Next time, South would play the ♡A and if West showed out, as in the diagram above, there would be a marked finesse against East.

By ducking on the first round of trumps, declarer makes certain that the contract is where it should be—in the bag.

YOUR MOVE

Dealer South: Both Vul:

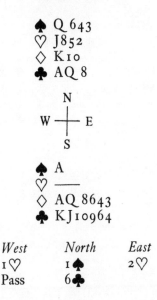

♠ Q 643
♡ J852
◇ K10
♣ AQ 8

N
W — E
S

♠ A
♡ ——
◇ AQ 8643
♣ KJ10964

South	West	North	East
1 ◇	1 ♡	1 ♠	2 ♡
5 ♣	Pass	6 ♣	

CONTRACT 6♣: LEAD ♡3

North is a sterling partner. The dummy he puts down, with all the high cards in just the right places, is much better than South had any right to expect. How should he make the most of it.?

East plays the ♡10 on dummy's ♡2.

THE AFTERMATH

```
                    ♠ Q 643
                    ♡ J852
                    ◇ K10
                    ♣ AQ 8

    ♠ J952          N          ♠ K1087
    ♡ AK9743                   ♡ Q 106
    ◇ —       W —|— E          ◇ J9752
    ♣ 752           S          ♣ 3

                    ♠ A
                    ♡ —
                    ◇ AQ 8643
                    ♣ KJ10964
```

Declarer drew trumps and continued with a low diamond. When West showed out, there was nothing South could do to avoid losing two diamonds.

Bad luck? Certainly, but surely not unexpected. West's lead of the ♡3 was ominous. With the ♡KQ or AK, he would have led the ♡K, unless he had good reason to do otherwise. Besides it isn't likely that he made a vulnerable overcall on a diaphanous four-card suit.

It looks very much as if West has daringly underled his tops to put East in with a view to a diamond ruff.

HAPPY ENDING

Fortunately, South can guard against a 5–0 diamond break. When East shows out on the second round of trumps, declarer crosses to the ♠A and leads a low diamond towards dummy. It wouldn't help for West to ruff, so he throws a heart. Declarer puts on dummy's ◇K and continues with the ◇10, which East covers—and South ducks!

Since East has no trump to play, no one can stop South from setting up his diamonds with one ruff in dummy.

YOUR MOVE

Dealer South: Love All

```
            ♠ 73
            ♡ 642
            ◇ 1076
            ♣ AK1087
                N
          W ──┼── E
                S
            ♠ AKQJ104
            ♡ AJ103
            ◇ A
            ♣ Q9
```

South	North
2♣	3♣
3♠	3NT
6♠	

CONTRACT 6♠ : LEAD ◇4

East goes up with the ◇K. Declarer has eleven top tricks. How should he play to give himself the best chance of making a twelfth?

THE AFTERMATH

```
                    ♠ 73
                    ♡ 642
                    ◇ 1076
                    ♣ AK1087
      ♠ 96              N          ♠ 852
      ♡ K85                        ♡ Q97
      ◇ Q954      W ─┼─ E          ◇ KJ832
      ♣ J632           S           ♣ 54
                    ♠ AKQJ104
                    ♡ AJ103
                    ◇ A
                    ♣ Q9
```

Declarer reeled off five spades in quick succession, just to make himself thoroughly disagreeable to opponents, but nothing much happened. East threw three diamonds. West parted with two diamonds and a heart.

South tested the clubs, and when the ♣J didn't come down, he turned to the hearts. He could still have made his contract had East turned up with a doubleton honour or with both honours.

South held his head high as he went down, for he felt that he had given himself every chance.

HAPPY ENDING

Declarer can hold his head still higher and make the contract.

He can take four rounds of trumps if he likes, but while he still has two left he should lead the ♣9 and overtake with the ♣10 in dummy. If East wins, there is no further problem. The ♣Q is overtaken by the ♣A and three hearts are parked on the clubs. If the ♣10 holds, South leads a heart to his ♡10. It is West's trick, but South has a second club entry in dummy for a finesse against East's ♡Q.

As before, declarer makes his contract if the ♣J comes down in three rounds or if East has both the ♡K and ♡Q, but he makes it also if the heart honours are divided.

YOUR MOVE

Dealer North: N/S Vul:

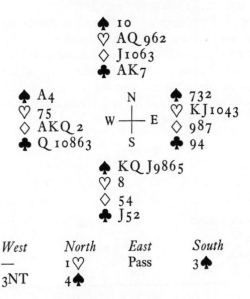

West	North	East	South
—	1♡	Pass	3♠
3NT	4♠		

CONTRACT 4♠: LEAD ◇K

West's 3NT was intended to elicit East's longer minor. The sacrifice wouldn't have been a great success, expecially if North-South could be defeated in 4♠.

Seeing all four hands, would you rather be South or West?

THE AFTERMATH

On West's $\diamondsuit$ K, East played the $\diamondsuit$ 7 and on the $\diamondsuit$ Q, which came next, he followed with the $\diamondsuit$ 9.

Reading this sequence as showing three diamonds and an interest in hearts, West switched to a heart at trick three.

Declarer went up with dummy's $\heartsuit$ A and drove out West's $\spadesuit$ A. He ruffed the heart return, and after drawing trumps, he crossed to the $\clubsuit$ A, to ruff another heart. The $\heartsuit$ K didn't appear, so South led out his trumps. When the last one hit the table, this was the position:

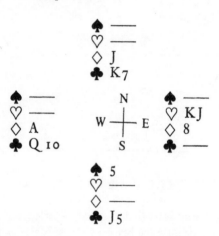

West was squeezed inexorably in the minors.

HAPPY ENDING—FOR WEST

West should see the danger of a squeeze looming ahead.

If East has a heart trick, it won't evaporate. So West continues with a third round of diamonds. South ruffs and dummy's $\diamondsuit$ J is master—but only for a moment. West comes in again with the $\spadesuit$ A and leads his last diamond. Partner ruffs dummy's $\diamondsuit$ J and there is longer a squeeze.

YOUR MOVE

Dealer West: Both Vul:

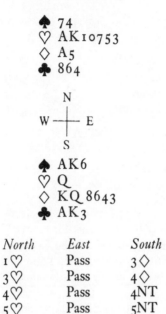

♠ 74
♡ A K 10 7 5 3
♢ A 5
♣ 8 6 4

N
W —┼— E
S

♠ A K 6
♡ Q
♢ K Q 8 6 4 3
♣ A K 3

West	North	East	South
Pass	1 ♡	Pass	3 ♢
Pass	3 ♡	Pass	4 ♢
Pass	4 ♡	Pass	4NT
Pass	5 ♡	Pass	5NT
Pass	6 ♢	Pass	6NT

CONTRACT 6NT: LEAD ♣ J

Surely South was pusilanimous to stop short of a grand slam. What more does he want?

Lucky for him that this isn't a duplicate pairs event, for he might be heading for something uncommonly like a bottom.

Fortunately, this is rubber bridge. The stakes are high, as usual, and a vulnerable small slam brings with it a rich reward—providing that it is made.

How should South attend to this detail?

THE AFTERMATH

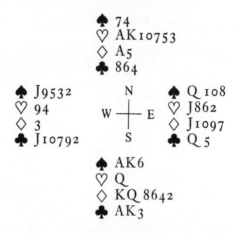

```
                    ♠ 74
                    ♡ A K 10 7 5 3
                    ◇ A 5
                    ♣ 8 6 4
     ♠ J 9 5 3 2        N        ♠ Q 10 8
     ♡ 9 4          W ─┼─ E      ♡ J 8 6 2
     ◇ 3               S         ◇ J 10 9 7
     ♣ J 10 7 9 2                ♣ Q 5
                    ♠ A K 6
                    ♡ Q
                    ◇ K Q 8 6 4 2
                    ♣ A K 3
```

With so many tricks about, South played quickly, without so much as one look at the ceiling. He cashed the ♡ Q, crossed to dummy with the ◇ A and led the ♡ A and ♡ K, discarding a spade and a club from his hand. The ♡ J didn't come down, but that wasn't serious for the diamonds were still there—or so it seemed.

Even with the unlucky diamond break, all would have been well had East not had the ♡ J to cash when he came in with his fourth diamond.

South was certainly very unlucky, but he could have twisted Dame Fortune's arm and made his contract just the same.

HAPPY ENDING

Having cashed the ♡ Q, he leads the ◇ 2—and ducks in dummy. He loses a diamond as before, but nothing else, for the ♡ AK haven't yet been cashed.

Whatever East returns, South goes over to the ◇ A, takes the two top hearts and spreads his hand.

YOUR MOVE

Dealer North: Both Vul:

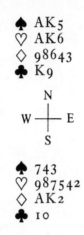

♠ AK5
♡ AK6
◇ 98643
♣ K9

```
        N
   W ──┼── E
        S
```

♠ 743
♡ 987542
◇ AK2
♣ 10

West	North	East	South
—	1◇	Pass	1♡
1♠	2♠	Pass	3◇
Pass	3♡	Pass	4♡

CONTRACT 4♡ : LEAD ♠J

This is a teams-of-four match.

The play to the first two tricks is the same in both rooms. The ♠J is taken by the ♠A, and the ♡A comes next. West discards the ♣2.

You are South in the Open Room, a vast audience watching you on Bridgerama.

What will they see you do?

THE AFTERMATH

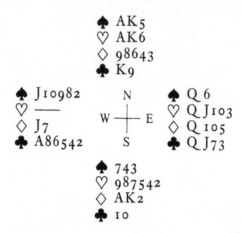

```
                    ♠ AK5
                    ♡ AK6
                    ◇ 98643
                    ♣ K9
   ♠ J10982        N            ♠ Q6
   ♡ —                          ♡ QJ103
   ◇ J7         W —┼— E         ◇ Q105
   ♣ A86542        S            ♣ QJ73
                    ♠ 743
                    ♡ 987542
                    ◇ AK2
                    ♣ 10
```

In the Closed Room, South cashed the ♡K and crossing to
his hand with a diamond, led a club. Despite his ♣2 at trick
one, West was pretty well marked with the ♣A on his bid, so
declarer's diamond loser was parked on the ♣K and the contract was defeated by only one trick.

"No swing here", said North confidently. Of course, he was
reckoning without you playing on Bridgerama.

HAPPY ENDING

Leaving trumps strictly alone, after the ♡A had revealed
the 4–0 break, you crossed to your hand with the ◇A and
cashed the ◇K, as well, the key play. Then, like South in the
closed room, you led a club setting up dummy's ♣K.

West led a second spade, but you were now in command.
Going up with the ♠K, you cashed the ♣K and discarded
your diamond. Now you ruffed a diamond, setting up the suit,
and going over to the ♡A, you threw your spade loser on a
diamond.

The defence could take no more than two trumps and the
♣A. A swing of 720 to your side.

YOUR MOVE

Dealer South: Love All

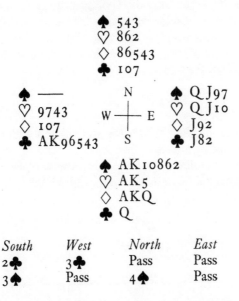

South	West	North	East
2♣	3♣	Pass	Pass
3♠	Pass	4♠	Pass

CONTRACT 4♠ : LEAD ♣K

As West continues with the ♣A, the kibitzers, seeing all four hands, quickly lose interest. Declarer has four inescapable losers—two trumps, a club and a heart.

If dummy had a couple of entries, East could be kept to one trump trick, but as dummy hasn't even one entry, what can poor South do?

What would you do in his place?

THE AFTERMATH

Nine declarers out of ten, and the tenth one, too, most of the time, will ruff the second club, lay down the ♠A, and seeing West show out, surrender gracefully—or not so gracefully.

And yet the seemingly impossible shouldn't be so lightly dismissed. Some of the time, when he is at his best, the tenth declarer will ensure a . . .

HAPPY ENDING

As a technician, he will ruff the second club with the ♠6, guarding jealously the ♠2, just in case. One never knows. Learning the bad news as he lays down the ♠A, he will cash the five winners in his side suits and exit with the ♡5, leaving this position:

```
              ♠ 54
              ♡ ──
              ◇ 86
              ♣ ──

   ♠ ──          N          ♠ QJ9
   ♡ J                       ♡ ──
   ◇ ──      W ──┼── E       ◇ ──
   ♣ 965          S          ♣ J

              ♠ K1082
              ♡ ──
              ◇ ──
              ♣ ──
```

Coming in with the ♡Q, East leads the ♠Q. South lets it hold, throwing the ♠8. East switches to the ♣J and now South reaps the reward for his technique at trick one. He ruffs with the ♠2, over-ruffs in dummy and leads a diamond through East's ♠J9 up to his ♠K10.

YOUR MOVE

Dealer South: Love All

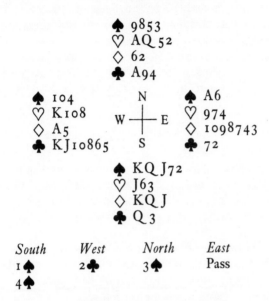

♠ 9853
♡ AQ52
♢ 62
♣ A94

♠ 104
♡ K108
♢ A5
♣ KJ10865

N
W — E
S

♠ A6
♡ 974
♢ 1098743
♣ 72

♠ KQJ72
♡ J63
♢ KQJ
♣ Q3

South	West	North	East
1♠	2♣	3♠	Pass
4♠			

CONTRACT 4♠: LEAD ♢A

Declarer wins the diamond continuation and plays a trump to East's ace. A third diamond is ruffed by West with the ♠ 10. Which side will you back?

What should declarer discard from dummy on the ♠ 10?

THE AFTERMATH

Did South discard dummy's ♣4? Then West exited with
the ♣K, which was worth a trick to declarer. The heart finesse
succeeded as expected, but there was no way of avoiding a
heart loser. One down.

But maybe South threw the ♡2 on that ♠10 at trick four.
West this time exited with a heart, but though declarer now
had no heart loser, he couldn't avoid giving up a club. As before,
one down.

HAPPY ENDING

Declarer knows that West's return will present him with a
trick in clubs or in hearts, though he doesn't know in which
suit it will be. Either way, he will still have to dispose of another
loser and the only hope is to squeeze West, who is marked with
both the ♡K and ♣K on his bid.

So South under-ruffs in dummy! Now he has menaces
against West in both hearts and clubs. West returns the ♣K—
he can no longer afford to lead a heart—and after taking the
heart finesse, declarer reaches this position:

```
                    ♠ ——
                    ♡ A5
                    ◇ ——
                    ♣ 9

     ♠ ——              N              ♠ ——
     ♡ K10                             ♡ 97
     ◇ ——       W ——+—— E             ◇ 9
     ♣ J              S               ♣ ——

                    ♠ 2
                    ♡ J6
                    ◇ ——
                    ♣ ——
```

On the ♠2 West is squeezed.

YOUR MOVE

Dealer South: N/S Vul:

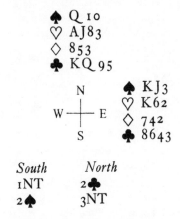

```
        ♠ Q 10
        ♡ AJ83
        ◇ 853
        ♣ KQ 95

          N          ♠ KJ3
                     ♡ K62
      W ──┼── E      ◇ 742
          S          ♣ 8643
```

South　　*North*
1NT　　　　2♣
2♠　　　　3NT

CONTRACT 3NT: LEAD ◇J

South wins with the ◇A and runs the ♡Q. West follows with the ♡4.

Is there any hope for the defence and, if so, what can East do, when he comes in with the ♡K, to bring about declarer's undoing?

THE AFTERMATH

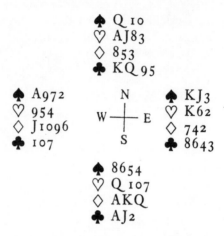

```
            ♠ Q 10
            ♡ AJ83
            ◇ 853
            ♣ KQ95

♠ A972          N          ♠ KJ3
♡ 954      W ──┼── E       ♡ K62
◇ J1096         S          ◇ 742
♣ 107                      ♣ 8643

            ♠ 8654
            ♡ Q 107
            ◇ AKQ
            ♣ AJ2
```

East could see that a diamond return would do no good, for declarer's play at trick one showed that he must have the ◇ AKQ. So, hoping for the best, he switched to the ♠ 3, a lucky strike—up to a point.

West won with the ♠ A and played back the ♠ 2. Having to concede three spades and a heart, declarer was kept to nine tricks, and East-West felt that they hadn't done too badly.

Seeing that dummy, opposite a strong 1NT, they had never fancied their chances. And yet East had the opportunity to break the contract.

HAPPY ENDING

West was marked with four spades—South's response to Stayman having shown four—and he had to have an ace; otherwise South would have had 20 points, too much for 1NT. The only hope was that West had the ♠ A, not the ♣ A. But to break the contract it was necessary for West to have something else as well—not an honour card, for there was no room for that, but the lowly, yet precious ♠ 9, flanked by the ♠ 7 or ♠ 8.

Coming in with the ♡ K, East switches to the ♠ J. West

wins, returns the ♠ 2 to East's ♠ K, picking up dummy's ♠ Q on the way, and now the ♠ 3 through the closed hand yields the defence two more tricks.

South's thoughtless play of the ◇ A at trick one puts the defence on the right track. If he wins with the ◇ K (or ◇ Q), East might place his partner with the ◇ A and treat the ◇ J as the top of an interior sequence.

YOUR MOVE

Dealer South: Love All

```
              ♠ 752
              ♡ 765
              ◇ AQ J10
              ♣ Q 53

              N
        W ——+—— E
              S

              ♠ K84
              ♡ AK9432
              ◇ K52
              ♣ A
```

South	North
1♡	1NT
3♡	4♡

CONTRACT 4♡ : LEAD ♣J

What should be declarer's plan of campaign ?

THE AFTERMATH

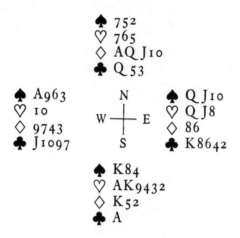

```
            ♠ 752
            ♡ 765
            ◇ AQ J10
            ♣ Q 53
♠ A963          N          ♠ Q J10
♡ 10      W ──┼── E        ♡ Q J8
◇ 9743          S          ◇ 86
♣ J1097                    ♣ K8642
            ♠ K84
            ♡ AK9432
            ◇ K52
            ♣ A
```

The ♣J, ♣3, ♣8 and ♣A made up the first trick. Declarer laid down the ♡A and ♡K and sighed deeply when West showed out. A little bird told him that things would go wrong. The little bird was right, but it was too late to catch the worm.

Hoping to get rid of a spade before losing the lead to East, declarer turned to the diamonds. East, however, ruffed on the third round and the ♠Q, through the closed hand, sealed South's fate.

HAPPY ENDING

Technically, at trick one, South should have covered the ♣J, to encourage a club continuation. More important, he should have tried to keep East out of the lead while he drew trumps.

At trick two declarer crosses to the ◇Q, leads a heart and inserts the ♡9. West wins, but a spade from him can do no harm and all is well.

If East splits his honours, declarer goes up with the ♡A, returns to dummy and again leads a trump through East. So long as East doesn't hold all three heart honours, the contract is safe.

YOUR MOVE

Dealer South: Both Vul:

```
              ♠ 85
              ♡ Q J642
              ◇ Q 63
              ♣ J74

                    N
              W ───┼─── E
                    S

              ♠ AKJ1097
              ♡ A3
              ◇ A2
              ♣ Q65
```

South	North
1♠	1NT
4♠	

CONTRACT 4♠: LEAD ♣K

East followed with the ♣2 and West quickly switched to the ◇10, covered by the ◇Q and ◇K, and won by South with the ◇A.

Which card should declarer lead at trick three?

Can South make the contract if East has the ♡K and:

(a) ♠ Q64?
(b) ♠ Q642?

THE AFTERMATH

```
                    ♠ 85
                    ♡ Q J642
                    ◇ Q 63
                    ♣ J74

    ♠ 3                  N          ♠ Q 642
    ♡ 975                           ♡ K108
    ◇ 109854      W ─┼─ E           ◇ KJ7
    ♣ AK108              S          ♣ 832

                    ♠ AKJ1097
                    ♡ A3
                    ◇ A2
                    ♣ Q 65
```

Coming in at trick two with the ◇ A, declarer played the ♣ Q . West held off. He won the next club and continued with the ◇ 9 and ◇ 5. Declarer ruffed and tried to drop the ♠ Q, though even that wouldn't have been enough to save the contract.

When East came in on the third round of trumps, he still had a trump left as a safe exit card and South had to concede a heart for two down.

A little forethought on South's part would have ensured a . . .

HAPPY ENDING

The urgency of an entry to dummy was self-evident, but fortunately for South the opening lead gave him a chance to create one.

Jettisoning the ♣ Q on the ♣ K, South wins the next trick, as before, with the ◇ A and continues with a low club. West goes up with his ♣ A, scores a diamond and leads another.

As declarer ruffs, he must use a speck of forethought, playing the ♠ 9, not the ♠ 7. The ♣ J provides the vital entry to dummy, allowing declarer to take the heart finesse. If East covers, dummy has another entry. If not, the lead remains in dummy and that is where South is rewarded for his forethought in retaining the ♠ 7. He can play it under dummy's ♠ 8 and again finesse against East.

So long as East has the ♡ K – and it isn't bare – South can make his contract, even against the 4–1 trump break.

YOUR MOVE

Dealer West: Love All

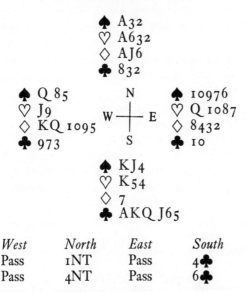

```
              ♠ A32
              ♡ A632
              ◇ AJ6
              ♣ 832
♠ Q 85         N        ♠ 10976
♡ J9                    ♡ Q 1087
◇ KQ 1095   W ─┼─ E     ◇ 8432
♣ 973          S        ♣ 10
              ♠ KJ4
              ♡ K54
              ◇ 7
              ♣ AKQ J65
```

West	North	East	South
Pass	1NT	Pass	4♣
Pass	4NT	Pass	6♣

CONTRACT 6♣: LEAD ◇K

A very suitable hand for the Gerber convention. South wants to keep out of a slam if North has one ace only, so he puts the question: how many aces have you, partner?

Had North replied 4♡, showing one ace, South could have stopped safely in 5♣

With two aces opposite—a 4♠ reply on Gerber—South would have still bid 6♣, for North would have had compensating values somewhere and the opening lead would run up to South. No danger there.

What is the best way to play the hand in 6♣?

THE AFTERMATH

The spade finesse wouldn't run away and neither would a 3–3 heart break. Meanwhile, South wanted to prepare the ground for a squeeze. So he played low from dummy at trick one, to rectify the count.

West switched to a trump. After two more rounds of trumps, declarer cashed the ♡K and ♡A, discarded a heart on the ◇A and ruffed a heart.

The hearts didn't split 3–3, but had West been long in the suit he would have been the victim of a squeeze. As he followed to the last trump he would have come down to three cards, and playing before dummy, he would have to keep the ◇Q and a heart, leaving room for one spade only. Picking it up with the ♠A, South would then take the marked finesse against East's ♠Q.

When, however, East showed up with the fourth heart, South abandoned the idea of a squeeze and staked his all on the spade finesse. One down.

HAPPY ENDING

South gave up his squeeze plan too soon. If East has to look after the hearts, he, too, becomes vulnerable.

This is the four-card end position:

```
              ♠ A 3
              ♡ 6
              ◇ J
              ♣ —
   ♠ Q 8 5        N        ♠ 1097
   ♡ —                     ♡ Q
   ◇ Q       W  —┼—  E     ◇ —
   ♣ —            S        ♣ —
              ♠ K J 4
              ♡ —
              ◇ —
              ♣ 6
```

On the ♣6, to keep the ◇Q, West must let go the spade. Having served its purpose, the ◇J is now thrown from dummy and the spotlight switches to East. What will he do?

The ♡6 is still in dummy, so East, too, has to part with a spade. South now knows that each defender, in turn, has a red card and that the ♠Q must drop.

YOUR MOVE

Dealer South: Both Vul:

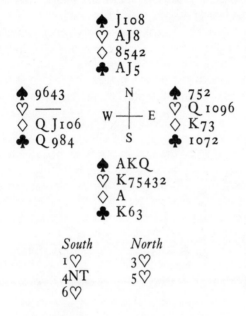

♠ J108
♡ AJ8
◇ 8542
♣ AJ5

♠ 9643   N   ♠ 752
♡ —   ♡ Q 1096
◇ QJ106 W—E ◇ K73
♣ Q984   S   ♣ 1072

♠ AKQ
♡ K75432
◇ A
♣ K63

South	North
1♡	3♡
4NT	5♡
6♡	

CONTRACT 6♡ : LEAD ◇Q

Without the benefit of seeing all four hands, which card should South lead at trick two?

And now you can look into your crystal. Peering through the vapours, can you see whether or not South will find a way to bring home his contract?

Yes, he can play double-dummy.

THE AFTERMATH

At trick two South led the ♡ K. When West showed out, prospects looked bleak, but there was still a chance if East could be end-played in trumps.

So South cashed his spades, successfully negotiated the club finesse and ruffed a diamond. The ♣ K and ♣ A followed and another diamond was ruffed in the closed hand.

The fourth diamond would now end-play East, but declarer was in his hand and dummy had no more entries.

HAPPY ENDING

South chose to lead the ♡ K in case West had all four trumps. The idea was sound, but it could have been given effect just as easily by leading a low heart. If East shows out, declarer gets back to his hand and leads low again to dummy's ♡ J.

Either way, West is kept to one trump trick. But observe the difference. Seeing West show out on the first heart, South goes up with the ♡ A and ruffs a diamond. He takes his spades and, as before, finesses the ♣ J and ruffs another diamond. The ♣ K comes next, then a club to dummy's ♣ A and this is the position:

```
                    ♠ —
                    ♡ J8
                    ◇ 8
                    ♣ —
        ♠ 9               N            ♠ —
        ♡ —                            ♡ Q 109
        ◇ J         W —┼— E           ◇ —
        ♣ Q               S            ♣ —
                    ♠ —
                    ♡ K75
                    ◇ —
                    ♣ —
```

The ◇ 8 is played from dummy. East ruffs and South *under-ruffs*. East must now play away from his ♡ Q.

YOUR MOVE

Dealer South: Love All

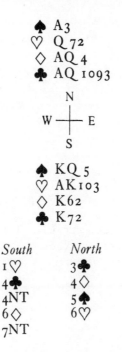

♠ A3
♡ Q 72
♢ AQ 4
♣ AQ 1093

```
        N
   W ───┼─── E
        S
```

♠ KQ 5
♡ AK103
♢ K62
♣ K72

South	North
1♡	3♣
4♣	4♢
4NT	5♠
6♢	6♡
7NT	

CONTRACT 7NT: LEAD ♠J

Years ago it didn't take so long to reach a grand slam on a combined 36 count, plus a good five-card suit. These days, we are more scientific and South realised that a really sophisticated bidder might well have found two more bids on the way. Still, he hadn't done so badly.

What card should South not play at trick two?

THE AFTERMATH

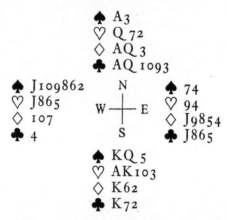

```
                    ♠ A3
                    ♡ Q72
                    ◇ AQ3
                    ♣ AQ 1093
   ♠ J109862           N           ♠ 74
   ♡ J865                           ♡ 94
   ◇ 107         W —┼— E            ◇ J9854
   ♣ 4                S             ♣ J865
                    ♠ KQ5
                    ♡ AK103
                    ◇ K62
                    ♣ K72
```

South could count thirteen tricks providing that the clubs didn't break 4–1. So at trick two, he led a club to dummy's ♣A and then another club to his ♣K. That way he could catch the ♣J even if West had four clubs.

When West threw a spade on the ♣K, things began to look grim. The only remaining hope was to bring in four hearts, but West was in no trouble with his discards and it didn't take South so long to lose his grand slam as it had taken him to bid it.

Had South not led a club, any club, at trick two, the story might have had a . . .

HAPPY ENDING

There can be no hurry to test the clubs. To gain information declarer should first explore the side suits.

The third round of spades reveals that West had six. Next he shows up with four hearts. That is ten cards in the majors. South continues with the ◇A and ◇K. If West follows both times, he cannot have more than one club. Declarer leads dummy's ♣A, to guard against a singleton ♣J, then runs the ♣10 in the knowledge that, unless East covers, it must win.

Dummy retains the ◇Q as an entry. Should West show out on the second round of diamonds, he must have two clubs, so all is well.

YOUR MOVE

Dealer South: E/W Vul:

```
            ♠ K102
            ♡ Q832
            ◇ AQ 104
            ♣ Q7
                N
         W  ──┼── E
                S
            ♠ AQ
            ♡ J10764
            ◇ KJ973
            ♣ 4
```

South	North
1♡	4♡

CONTRACT 4♡ : LEAD ◇2

What is declarer's main problem and how should he seek to solve it?

The reader is entitled to a clue. This hand is not quite so straightforward as most of those that have gone before. To find the answer will require imagination, as well as technique.

THE AFTERMATH

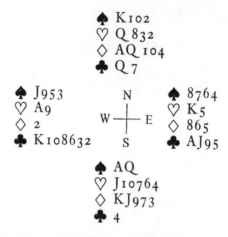

Declarer realised that the ◇ 2 was, could only be, a singleton. His main problem was, therefore, to avoid a ruff. Hoping that the heart honours would be divided, he won the first trick in the closed hand, and led a low trump.

If West plays low, declarer is out of the wood, for it won't hurt him to have a diamond ruffed with the ♡ A (or ♡ K).

West, however, went up promptly with the ♡ A, put East in with the ♣ A and ruffed the diamond return.

HAPPY ENDING

Recognising the danger of a diamond ruff, South shouldn't draw trumps until he has severed communications between East and West. There is nothing he can do if East holds the ♡ AK, but if the honours are divided, South gives himself an extra chance by trying the Scissors Coup.

Before touching trumps he leads the ♠ A, then the ♠ Q and overtakes with the ♠ K in dummy. Next comes the ♠ 10 and—unless East has the ♠ J—South discards his singleton club.

West can no longer put East in to give him that diamond ruff.

YOUR MOVE

Dealer South: Game All

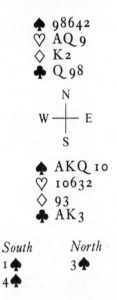

♠ 98642
♡ AQ 9
◇ K 2
♣ Q 98

```
        N
    W ──┼── E
        S
```

♠ AKQ 10
♡ 10632
◇ 93
♣ AK 3

South	*North*
1 ♠	3 ♠
4 ♠	

CONTRACT 4♠ : LEAD ◇Q

Trumps break 2–2 and there are no voids about.
How should South play to make certain of his contract?

THE AFTERMATH

```
                    ♠ 98642
                    ♡ AQ 9
                    ◇ K2
                    ♣ Q 98
   ♠ J3              N              ♠ 75
   ♡ 743                            ♡ KJ8
   ◇ QJ106      W ─┼─ E             ◇ A8754
   ♣ 10762          S               ♣ J54
                    ♠ AKQ 10
                    ♡ 10632
                    ◇ 93
                    ♣ AK 3
```

South covered the ◇ Q in dummy and lost the trick to
East's ◇ A. The ◇ 8, clearly a suit preference signal, came
back to the ◇ 10 and West duly switched to the ♡ 7.

Declarer played the ♡ 9 from dummy, but he couldn't
avoid losing another heart and finished one down.

HAPPY ENDING

South can ensure his contract against anything an unkind
fate may do by playing low from dummy at trick one. Obviously,
West hasn't made an acrobatic lead of the ◇ Q from ◇ AQ,
so South has nothing to gain—and much to lose—by covering.
Observe what happens if he doesn't.

If West switches at trick two to a heart, South goes up with
the ♡ A, draws trumps, cashes the clubs and throws East in
with the ◇ A.

If West continues with a second diamond to East's ◇ A,
South is put to even less trouble. He wins the next trick, a club
or a spade, and as before draws trumps and eliminates clubs.
Then he leads a heart, inserting the ♡ 9 from dummy. East is
end-played.

YOUR MOVE

Dealer South: Love All

♠ J762
♡ A5
◇ KQJ
♣ K984

N
W ─┼─ E
S

♠ AK1093
♡ 96
◇ 1043
♣ A52

South	North
1♠	2♣
2♠	4♠

CONTRACT 4♠: LEAD ♡K

Hearing South open proceedings with 1♠, North visualised possibilities of a slam. Not quite good enough to force, he tried the next best thing, a delayed game raise.

Had South's rebid been anything other than 2♠, North's jump to 4♠ would have conveyed the message, saying in effect:

"I must have four spades to bid this way. Why, then, didn't I support you at once? Because I am too good".

With extra values, South would have gone on.

Over a minimum rebid, North was happy to settle for game. How should South make it?

THE AFTERMATH

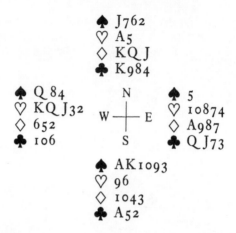

```
              ♠ J762
              ♡ A5
              ◇ KQJ
              ♣ K984

♠ Q84          N          ♠ 5
♡ KQJ32    W ──┼── E      ♡ 10874
◇ 652                     ◇ A987
♣ 106          S          ♣ QJ73

              ♠ AK1093
              ♡ 96
              ◇ 1043
              ♣ A52
```

It looks as if the contract depends on not losing a spade, and in the event, South lost a trick in each suit. One down.

He won the opening lead with dummy's ♡A, laid down the two top trumps and turned to the diamonds. Coming in with the ◇A, East returned a heart to West's ♡Q. West quickly cashed his ♠Q and exited with a diamond. Thereafter, declarer had no way of avoiding a club loser.

HAPPY ENDING

South can improve his chances by ducking on the first trick. It is the old story of disrupting enemy communications.

It matters little what West does next. Suppose that he continues hearts. Declarer takes one round of trumps and drives out the ◇A. Winning the club return, he takes a second round of trumps, cashes his second top club, and scores his two diamond winners. West is now put on play with the ♠Q and compelled to play a red suit, giving declarer a ruff and discard, just what he needs to get rid of that club.

Of course, West might have had a third club, but by playing him for a doubleton, South gives himself an extra chance.

YOUR MOVE

Dealer South: N/S Vul:

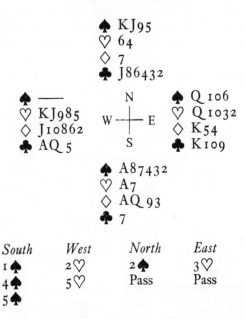

	♠ KJ95	
	♡ 64	
	◇ 7	
	♣ J86432	

```
              N
♠ —                    ♠ Q 106
♡ KJ985    W ─┼─ E     ♡ Q 1032
◇ J10862               ◇ K54
♣ AQ 5          S      ♣ K109

              ♠ A87432
              ♡ A7
              ◇ AQ 93
              ♣ 7
```

South	West	North	East
1 ♠	2 ♡	2 ♠	3 ♡
4 ♠	5 ♡	Pass	Pass
5 ♠			

CONTRACT 5♠ : LEAD ♡8

Declarer won with the ♡ A and decided, after due reflection, that he couldn't afford to lay down the ♠ A to cater for a 3–0 trump break.

So, at trick two, he crossed to the ♠ K, learned the bad news, and took the diamond finesse. After throwing dummy's heart on his ◇ A, he continued with the ♣ 7.

If you could place an even money bet, which side would you back?

THE AFTERMATH

Coming in with the ♣9 at trick five—after a heart, a spade and two rounds of diamonds—East exited with the ◇K.

Declarer had three trumps left in dummy to look after the three red losers, and despite the unlucky trump break, he made his contract. For all that, it was for the defence that the hand should have had a . . .

HAPPY ENDING

The spotlight is on East. When he comes in with his ♣9, he can beat the contract by returning the ♠Q. This is the position:

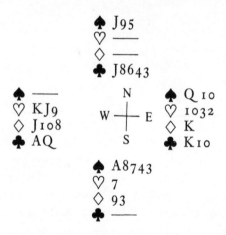

                    ♠ J95
                    ♡ —
                    ◇ —
                    ♣ J8643
        ♠ —   N   ♠ Q 10
        ♡ KJ9   ♡ 1032
        ◇ J108   W ─┼─ E   ◇ K
        ♣ AQ   S   ♣ K10
                    ♠ A8743
                    ♡ 7
                    ◇ 93
                    ♣ —

East sacrifices a certain trump trick—or so it seems—but he gets it back at once, for now declarer can only ruff two losers in dummy. And East still gets his trump trick. The ♠10 will score or else declarer will be kept to one ruff in dummy.

YOUR MOVE

Dealer South: N/S Game

♠ AQ
♡ 642
◊ 97654
♣ J72

N
W ─┼─ E
S

♠ 9642
♡ AK
◊ AK
♣ AQ 1096

South	*North*
1♣	1◊
3NT	

CONTRACT 3NT: LEAD ♠5

Do you expect declarer to make his contract if:
   (a) West has: ♠KJ10xx and ♣Kx?
   (b) East has the ♠K and West has the ♣Kx?
What is your plan?

THE AFTERMATH

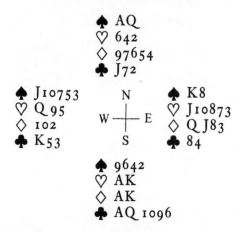

    ♠ AQ
    ♡ 642
    ◇ 97654
    ♣ J72

♠ J10753   N   ♠ K8
♡ Q95   ♡ J10873
◇ 102   W —|— E   ◇ QJ83
♣ K53   S   ♣ 84

    ♠ 9642
    ♡ AK
    ◇ AK
    ♣ AQ1096

South took the losing spade finesse and the spade return knocked out dummy's ♠ A. Declarer rightly laid down the ♣ A to cater for the bare ♣ K with West. The finesse would have served no purpose, for if East had the ♣ K, he could do no harm. Either he would have no spade to return or else, if he started with three, the spades were innocuous.

Finding West with five spades and the guarded ♣ K, South came off second best. Had he shown more forethought his contract would have had a . . .

HAPPY ENDING

South should have gone up with the ♠ A at trick one. This loses only if West has led the ♠ 5 from KJ10xx, which is unlikely. With that holding he would have probably preferred to lead the ♠ J, the top of his interior sequence.

If East has any one of the missing spade honours, the play of the ♠ A blocks the suit (if East has three spades, the suit isn't dangerous).

Having won the first trick with the ♠ A, declarer leads dummy's ♣ J and unblocks with the ♣ 9 from his hand. This is worth an extra trick if West has the singleton ♣ 8.

YOUR MOVE

Dealer West: Both Vul:

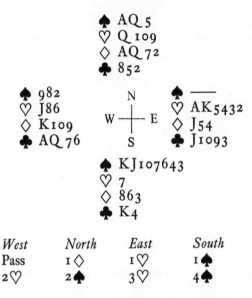

```
                    ♠ AQ 5
                    ♡ Q 109
                    ◇ AQ 72
                    ♣ 852

   ♠ 982            N            ♠ —
   ♡ J86                         ♡ AK5432
   ◇ K109        W —┼— E         ◇ J54
   ♣ AQ 76                       ♣ J1093
                    S
                    ♠ KJ107643
                    ♡ 7
                    ◇ 863
                    ♣ K4
```

West	North	East	South
Pass	1◇	1♡	1♠
2♡	2♠	3♡	4♠

CONTRACT 4♠ : LEAD ♡6

Declarer inserted the ♡9 from dummy and lost to East's ♡K. Switching to a club at trick two, defenders took two more tricks. Then declarer came in by ruffing a third club.

You are South. Are you going to make your contract?

THE AFTERMATH

The play to the first trick pinpoints the heart position. Since dummy's ♡9 brought the ♡K from East, West must have the ♡J, and if the ♡6 was his lowest, he cannot have more than three hearts.

If East had the ◇K, there would be no story to tell, so you assume—you are South, remember—that West has the ◇K. As you are in a position to build up an accurate picture of the entire deal, you are entitled to play double-dummy.

Despite the success of the diamond finesse, there is still an inescapable diamond loser, and with anyone else at the wheel, the contract goes one down. With you in charge, the inescapable loser escapes and the hand has a . . .

HAPPY ENDING

Having ruffed the third club, you play four rounds of spades, coming to this five-card end position:

```
                    ♠ —
                    ♡ Q 10
                    ◇ A Q 7
                    ♣ —

    ♠ —                 N                ♠ —
    ♡ J8                              ♡ A5
    ◇ K109      W ——— E            ◇ J54
    ♣ —                 S                ♣ —

                    ♠ 107
                    ♡ —
                    ◇ 863
                    ♣ —
```

You lead the ♠10, compelling West to let go a diamond. Otherwise you would take the diamond finesse and play the ♡Q, forcing East's ♡A and scooping West's ♡J.

A diamond is thrown from dummy and now East is in trouble.

Since he cannot afford to bare the ♡A, he, too, parts with a diamond. The diamond finesse follows, the ◇A is cashed and the ♠7 and ◇8 score the last two tricks.

An early diamond switch by the defence might have upset the applecart, but why worry about that now?

YOUR MOVE

Dealer West: Both Vul:

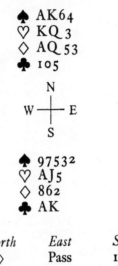

♠ AK64
♡ KQ 3
◇ AQ 53
♣ 105

```
        N
   W ——┼—— E
        S
```

♠ 97532
♡ AJ5
◇ 862
♣ AK

West	North	East	South
Pass	1 ◇	Pass	1 ♠
Pass	4 ♠	Pass	5 ♣
Pass	5 ◇	Pass	5 ♡
Pass	6 ♠		

CONTRACT 6♠: LEAD ♣Q

South certainly left nothing unsaid: Given a little more space, he would have probably shown his ♡ J as well.

The situation, unpromising from the start, deteriorates further when West throws a club on the second round of trumps.

How should declarer continue?

THE AFTERMATH

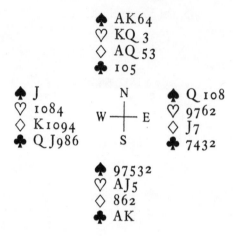

Declarer cashed his second club, took his three hearts and exited with a spade to East's ♠ Q. Instead of the good fortune he needed to bring home a daring contract, he had found an unlucky trump break, but at least he wouldn't go more than one down, even if East had the ◇ K.

It was a defeatist policy, but evidently South was as pessimistic in his play as he was optimistic in his bidding.

Had he put on a pair of rose-coloured spectacles his unhappy contract might have had a . . .

HAPPY ENDING

Even had the trumps broken kindly, the diamond finesse would have had to be right. And if it is, there is no need to despair. To make up for the 3–1 trump break, South must find East with a doubleton diamond. Since the odds favour a 4–2 division, there is no special reason why East shouldn't be short in the suit.

Before throwing East in with the ♠ Q, declarer takes the diamond finesse and cashes the ◇ A. Now East is forced to concede a ruff and discard, and all is well.

YOUR MOVE

Dealer South: Both Vul:

♠ K83
♡ J103
◇ A852
♣ 864

```
        N
   W ──┼── E
        S
```

♠ A94
♡ K98
◇ K74
♣ AQJ10

South	North
1NT	2NT
3NT	

CONTRACT 3NT: LEAD ♡5

Declarer put up dummy's ♡J and East won with the ♡A.
South should have made his contract, but failed to spot the right play in time and went one down.
Where was the ♣K?
What was the correct play?

THE AFTERMATH

```
              ♠ K83
              ♡ J103
              ♢ A852
              ♣ 864

♠ QJ10          N           ♠ 7652
♡ Q7652                     ♡ A4
♢ Q109       W ─┼─ E        ♢ J63
♣ 72            S           ♣ K953

              ♠ A94
              ♡ K98
              ♢ K74
              ♣ AQJ10
```

Unless the club finesse succeeds, declarer cannot come to nine tricks. Since we are told that he should have made the contract, it follows that East must have the ♣ K. Why, then, did declarer go down? Because the ♣ K was guarded too well. This means that East had not less than four clubs. To make all his own four clubs, which he wanted for his contract, South needed three entries to dummy and he had two only, the ♠ K and the ♢ A.

HAPPY ENDING

South should have created a third entry in dummy by unblocking at trick one. On the ♡ A he should have thrown his ♡ K. Now dummy has an additional entry in hearts.

This play cannot lose. On the Rule of Eleven, West, who led the ♡ 5 (11 − 5 = 6), must have the ♡ Q, for South can see at trick one all six cards higher than the ♡ 5—two in dummy, three in his own hand and one, the ♡ A, with East.

West, incidentally, should have five hearts, for East returned the ♡ 4 and the ♡ 2 is missing.

YOUR MOVE

Dealer South: Love All

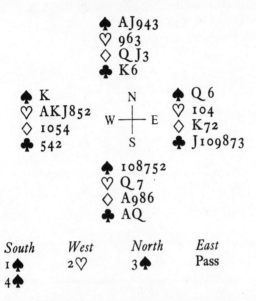

South	*West*	*North*	*East*
1♠	2♡	3♠	Pass
4♠			

CONTRACT 4♠: LEAD ♡K

West continued with the ♡ A and ♡ J. And now they are coming under starter's orders. So, to mix the metaphor, *Messieurs, faites vos jeux*.

Can South make his contract? Can East-West defeat him? They are off. *Rien ne va plus*.

THE AFTERMATH

On the third round of hearts East threw a club and declarer ruffed. The ♠A was followed by the ♣A and ♣K, and now East was thrown in with the ♠Q.

With six cards left, the position was:

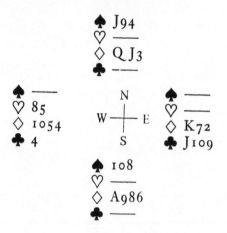

East was helpless. If he led a diamond, South's ◇8 would force West's ◇10 and East's ◇K would be exposed to a simple finesse.

A club return would allow declarer to ruff in his hand and throw the ◇3 from dummy. Again the ◇K would be doomed.

Did you back South? Unlucky. Inspired defence by East ensures for his side a . . .

HAPPY ENDING

At trick three East ruffs the ♡J with the ♠Q. At this stage he can exit safely with a club or with his other trump and the end-play won't take effect.

Should East find this defence?

In the post-mortem, certainly. In actual play, few Easts would think of it. And if South turned up with ♠Kxxx, fewer still would forgive themselves if they had.

YOUR MOVE

Dealer West: E/W Vul:

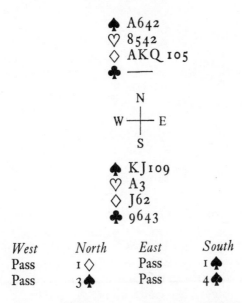

♠ A642
♡ 8542
♢ AKQ 105
♣ —

```
        N
    W —┼— E
        S
```

♠ KJ109
♡ A3
♢ J62
♣ 9643

West	North	East	South
Pass	1 ♢	Pass	1 ♠
Pass	3 ♠	Pass	4 ♠

CONTRACT 4♠ : LEAD ♣K

"So, we've missed it again", said South to himself, sorrow-fully, as dummy went down.

He could play either defender for the ♠Q, of course, but to keep control of the situation, he led a low spade from dummy at trick two—after ruffing the ♣K—and finessed against East, who followed with the ♠3.

South's ♠9 won. How should he continue?

THE AFTERMATH

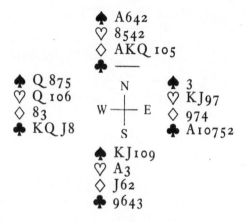

Having brought off the trump finesse, South could see twelve tricks before him more clearly than ever and he decided to speak severely to North about his unimaginative bidding. Meanwhile, he continued with a second trump to dummy's ace.

When East showed out, the hand suddenly collapsed.

South came back to his hand with the ◇ J and ruffed a club with dummy's last trump. Then he went on with the diamonds, but West ruffed on the third round and quickly cashed two clubs. There was still a heart to lose, so instead of missing a slam, South had the ignominy of going down in a mere game.

HAPPY ENDING

West produced a brilliant defence, but South should have ensured his contract.

Having finessed successfully against East, he should now finesse against West! When the ♠ 9 holds, he runs the ♠ 10. The worst that could happen would be for East to win and return a trump. Declarer still makes ten tricks with: three trumps, a club ruff, five diamonds and the ♡ A.

This is a difficult hand and many an expert would go down

on it. And yet, the reader with a retentive memory might well have found the solution, for the principle behind it has come up once before—to be precise on the first hand in the Collection. And what ending could be happier than going back to the beginning?